SMART CHOICES
Decision-Making for Kids

Matthew Black

Square Reads

Copyright © 2023 by Matthew Black

The content contained within this book may not be reproduced, duplicated, or transmitted without direct written permission from the author or the publisher.

Under no circumstances will any blame or legal responsibility be held against the publisher, or author, for any damages, reparation, or monetary loss due to the information contained within this book. Either directly or indirectly. You are responsible for your own choices, actions, and results.

Legal Notice:

This book is copyright protected. This book is only for personal use. You cannot amend, distribute, sell, use, quote or paraphrase any part, or the content within this book, without the consent of the author or publisher.

Disclaimer Notice:

Please note the information contained within this document is for educational and entertainment purposes only. All effort has been executed to present accurate, up-to-date, and reliable, complete information. No warranties of any kind are declared or implied.

Readers acknowledge that the author is not engaging in the rendering of legal, financial, medical or professional advice. The content within this book has been derived from various sources. Please consult a licensed professional before attempting any techniques outlined in this book.

By reading this document, the reader agrees that under no circumstances is the author responsible for any losses, direct or indirect, which are incurred as a result of the use of the information contained within this document, including, but not limited to, — errors, omissions, or inaccuracies.

First Edition

ISBN 978-1-7391181-7-4

Contents

Preface   VII
The Dilemma of Choices

1. Introduction to Making Smart Decisions   1
   What Is a Decision?
   Understanding Decision-Making

2. Why Is Decision-Making Important?   9
   Benefits of Making Smart Choices
   Consequences of Poor Decision-Making

3. The Decision-Making Process   15
   Identify the Decision
   Identifying Available Options

4. Gather Information   21
   Researching and Gathering Facts
   Seeking Advice From Trusted Sources

5. Evaluate Your Options   27
   Weighing the Pros and Cons
   Considering the Potential Outcomes

6. Making Your Choice   33
   Trusting Your Instincts
   Using Critical Thinking Skills

7. Take Action   39
   Implementing Your Decision
   Dealing With Possible Challenges

8. Sitting on the Fence   45

9. Factors Influencing Decision-Making   51
   Personal Values and Beliefs
   Understanding the Importance of Personal Values
   Exploring How Beliefs Can Impact Decisions

10. Emotions   57
    How Emotions Can Affect Decision-Making
    Strategies for Managing Emotions

11. Peer Pressure   63
    Recognizing Different Types of Peer Pressure
    Strategies for Resisting Negative Peer Pressure

12. Types of Decisions You May Encounter   69
    Choosing What to Wear
    Deciding What to Eat for Breakfast
    School-Related Decisions
    Selecting Extracurricular Activities
    Determining How to Study Effectively

13. Making Smart Decisions About Spending   79

14. Social Decisions   85
    Deciding Who to Be Friends With
    Handling Conflicts With Peers

15. Problem-Solving and Decision-Making   91
    Understanding the Connection Between Problems and Decisions
    Developing Problem-Solving Skills
    Using the Decision-Making Process for Solving Problems

      Examples of Problem-Solving Using Decision-Making Skills

16. Become a Decision-Maker Superhero   99
      Empowering You to Make Smart Choices

17. A Test of Friendship and Ethical Choices   107

18. Making Ethical Choices   111
      What Exactly Are Ethics?
      Considering the Impact of Decisions on Others
      Evaluating the Ethical Implications of Choices

19. Independent Decision-Making   119
      Understanding the Power of Choice

20. Impulsive Decisions   125
      Understanding Impulsive Decisions
      Triggers of Impulsive Decisions
      Cultivating Thoughtful Decision-Making
      Learning From Impulsive Choices

Conclusion   133
  Recap of Decision-Making Skills
  Reviewing the Decision-Making Process
  Helpful Tips

What Are Your Decisions?   141

Glossary   153

Preface

The Dilemma of Choices

First Scenario

Lily and Ethan were best friends who lived in a small town called Willowbrook. One sunny afternoon, they faced a life-changing situation while playing in their favorite park. Lily found a wallet filled with loads of cash under a tree. Excitement filled her as she thought of all the things they could buy and the fun they could have, but Ethan knew that keeping the wallet was wrong.

He suggested they should return it to its rightful owner, but Lily couldn't resist the temptation of spending all that money.

So they decided to keep the wallet and indulged in buying toys and treats. After a while, the guilt of their decision started to weigh heavily on Lily. Sleepless nights and a heavy heart haunted her, and the joy of their newfound wealth faded. As rumors of what they had done spread, their friends were disappointed to learn where their sudden fortune had come from.

Finally, Lily couldn't bear the burden anymore and approached Ethan with tears in her eyes. They decided to return the wallet and face the consequences. They confessed their wrongdoing to Mr. Thompson, the wallet's owner, and apologized. Despite feeling disappointed, Mr. Thompson forgave them, recognizing their courage and honesty.

From that day on, Lily and Ethan made better decisions and learned the value of honesty, integrity, and accountability. Their experience taught them that good decisions lead to personal growth and happiness, while bad decisions have consequences that can weigh heavily on one's heart.

Second Scenario

Lily and Ethan were well known for their unwavering friendship and integrity in the charming town of Willowbrook. One sunny day, they found a wallet filled with money in the park. Lily was thrilled about their unexpected luck, but Ethan reminded her that it belonged to someone else. Together, they decided to do the right thing and handed the wallet to the park authorities.

Their act of honesty touched the heart of Mr. Thompson, the wallet's owner, who had been desperately searching for it. He thanked Lily and Ethan for restoring his faith in goodness and kindness. When their teachers and parents heard what they had done, they applauded their exceptional character because they knew how tempting it would have been to have kept the money, and when they had faced the dilemma of choosing what to do, they had done the right thing.

As they grew older, their friendship remained strong, and they became natural leaders, inspiring others to make ethical choices. Even as they pursued different paths in college, they stayed true to their values. Lily and Ethan knew that making good decisions was an ongoing journey, and they were confident it would lead to a bright and promising future.

Impact of Different Decisions

In the first scenario, where Lily and Ethan decided to keep the money they found in the wallet, their lives became turbulent. The thrill of newfound wealth quickly faded, replaced by guilt, anxiety, and strained relationships. The weight of their dishonest decision haunted them day and night, making it difficult to enjoy the material possessions they had acquired. Their reputation suffered, and rumors spread, tarnishing the friendship that everybody admired.

The consequences of their bad decision extended beyond their personal lives, affecting Mr. Thompson, the rightful owner of the wallet. He experienced distress and financial burden due to the loss of his money. The community was disheartened to learn of Lily and Ethan's actions, questioning their integrity and trustworthiness.

On the other hand, in the second scenario, when Lily and Ethan chose to hand in the wallet and its contents to the park authorities, their lives took a different direction. Their decision to do the right thing showcased their integrity and strengthened their bond of friendship. Their selflessness inspired those around them, creating a positive ripple effect throughout the community.

They restored his faith in humanity by returning the wallet to Mr. Thompson. They reaffirmed the town's belief in the values that are important. Their reputation soared, and they became role models for their friends, setting an example of honesty and compassion.

The differences between the two scenarios lie in the outcomes of their decisions. In the first scenario, their wrong decision brought negative consequences, causing them immense guilt, damaging their reputation, and creating a sense of chaos in their lives. In contrast, in the second scenario, their good decision brought about positive consequences, instilling a sense of pride and fulfillment, deepening their friendships, and gaining the respect and admiration of their community.

These two scenarios serve as powerful life lessons on the significance of decision-making and its lasting impact. The choices we make not only define our character but also shape our relationships and influence the world around us. By demonstrating honesty, integrity, and compassion, Lily and Ethan revealed the profound influence of good decisions and the importance of considering the consequences of their actions.

As they venture into their future, the experiences of these two scenarios will continue to guide Lily and Ethan. They have learned that making wise and ethical choices may not always be easy, but the rewards of integrity and doing what is right far outweigh any temporary gains from dishonesty.

Their stories inspired others to be mindful of their decisions, understand the power of choice, and strive to make choices that align with the values that contribute positively to their lives and the world around them.

"Sometimes the hardest thing and the right thing are the same. Be brave, make your choice, and do what's right!"
- Anonymous

Chapter 1

Introduction to Making Smart Decisions

Have you ever found yourself in a situation where you have to make an important decision and found making the right choice difficult?

How do you know what to do?

In our everyday lives, we face countless choices – big and small. Should you play soccer or join the art club? Should you eat a healthy snack or a sugary treat?

These decisions may seem simple, but they can greatly impact your life. That's why learning how to make smart choices is important, especially when you're a kid.

Welcome to *Smart Choices: Decision-Making for Kids*!

Before we get into the content, you need to be congratulated on making the decision to read this book. There are probably other things you would prefer doing, like watching TV, playing a game, or spending time with your friends, and this may seem a little boring and unnecessary to you right now.

You may have been given the book to read and told how it would benefit you, or perhaps you chose to read it yourself. No matter how this book came to be in your hands, the first thing to note is that you decided to read it.

You made that decision!

As you go through this book, please think about how you decided to read it. What factors did you take into consideration? What were your reasons? This will become easier as you begin to understand all about decision-making, but for now, let's agree that you definitely made the smart choice!

At the back of the book is a Glossary. This contains a list of words that you may read in the book that you do not understand. If the word is there, you will be able to find out exactly what it means.

Before the Glossary, you will have the opportunity to make decisions in 30 hypothetical situations. This will give you the opportunity to use the knowledge you will learn in this book.

Some points in the book are intentionally discussed more than once. It's important that you don't assume you already know everything because although the information might sound similar to what you've read before, there may be a twist, or it will be explained differently.

By the end of this book, you will have all the knowledge and tools to guide you on your decision-making journey to ensure that you are fully equipped to make the right choices for your success.

Decision-making is a crucial life skill that will empower you to navigate various situations confidently and successfully throughout your life.

Together we will explore the importance of making smart choices and provide valuable tools to help you develop your decision-making skills.

In life, we are faced with decisions all the time. Some decisions are easy, like choosing what to wear or what to have for breakfast. But other decisions can be more challenging and have a bigger impact on our lives. That's why it's important to learn how to make smart choices.

What is a smart choice?

A smart choice is one that you think about carefully by considering all the options and consequences, to make the best decision for you. It's about thinking things through and not rushing into a decision.

Many factors can influence how a decision is made, and in this book, we will take a look at these.

But first, let's understand exactly what a decision is.

What Is a Decision?

Have you ever been faced with a choice and wondered what to do? That's when you have to make a decision!

A decision is when you choose between different options or possibilities. It's like picking the best path in a maze or deciding which flavor of ice cream to have – it's all about making a choice.

Decisions are a part of our everyday lives. We make decisions from the moment we wake up until we go to bed.

Some decisions are small, like choosing which shoes to wear or what snack to eat. Others are big, like choosing which sport to play or which subjects to take. No matter the size, each decision shapes our lives and helps us grow.

Decision-making can sometimes feel challenging, but there are smart ways to do it. First, it's important to gather information about your options. Let's say you want to buy a new toy. You can research different toys, ask friends or family for recommendations, and read reviews. The more you know, the better equipped you are to decide.

Next, think about what's important to you. Consider your values, interests, and goals. For example, a construction set might be your best choice if you love building things. If you enjoy drawing, an art kit might be more suitable. Knowing yourself and what you want can help you make decisions that align with your passions.

Another helpful tool is weighing the pros and cons of each option. List out the advantages and disadvantages, and consider how each choice will affect you in the short and long term. Doing this lets you see which option has more positives and which might have more drawbacks.

Lastly, trust your instincts.

Sometimes, our gut feelings can guide us in the right direction. Close your eyes, take a deep breath, and listen to your inner voice. What does it tell you? If something feels right, it's often a good sign that you're making a wise decision.

Remember making good decisions is a skill that gets better with practice. It's okay to make mistakes along the way – that's how we learn and grow.

So, embrace the power of decisions and learn all you can to ensure you start making choices that will positively shape your future.

In further chapters, everything you need to know will be explained in more detail, but first, let's begin by understanding more about decision-making in general.

Understanding Decision-Making

Have you ever wondered how to make good decisions?

To make good decisions, it's important first to understand what decision-making is all about.

Decision-making is the process of selecting the best option among different alternatives by considering the consequences of each choice.

Making informed decisions that align with your values, goals, and well-being is essential.

By learning how to make smart choices, you will develop a strong foundation for a successful future.

Identifying Choices

One essential skill that will help you become a better decision-maker is learning to identify and define the problem.

Sometimes, the choices we have to make to resolve the issue can seem overwhelming. By breaking down the decision into smaller parts and clearly understanding the problem, you can make the decision-making process much easier.

The first step in making smart choices is recognizing the available options, as every decision has multiple options, each with different outcomes. Developing this awareness will make you more confident in making informed decisions.

Evaluating Consequences

Another critical aspect of decision-making is considering the consequences. Every decision we make has results for now and in the future. It's important to think about what might happen because of our choices before we decide.

We can make smarter decisions that match our values and goals by considering the good and not-so-good outcomes.

Thinking about how each option will impact you and others involved will help you make more informed decisions.

Consider the risks and benefits of each choice, and think about what will make you happiest in the long run.

Gathering Information

Gathering information is also crucial in decision-making. The more information you have, the better equipped you are to make a good choice. Talk to people who have experience or knowledge about the decision you're making. Do some research, read books, or search the internet to gather as much information as possible. Knowledge is power when it comes to decision-making.

Making Ethical Decisions

Ethical decision-making is an integral part of making smart choices. Later in the book, we will discuss the importance of considering the ethical implications of our decisions and how they can impact ourselves and others.

You will show compassion and become more responsible by understanding the value of ethical decision-making.

Considering Alternatives

Sometimes, there is more than one right answer or solution to a problem. You will learn how to brainstorm and consider various alternatives when deciding. This skill will help you think creatively and find the best possible solution.

Trust Your Instincts

Lastly, trust your instincts. Sometimes, your gut feeling can guide you in the right direction. Listen to your inner voice and pay attention to any red flags or warning signs. Trust yourself and your ability to make good decisions.

Remember, decision-making is a skill that can be developed and improved over time, like any skill you have learned and practiced. You will become a confident decision-maker by understanding the process, defining the problem, considering the consequences, gathering information, and trusting your instincts.

So, next time you're faced with a choice, use the skills you are about to discover to make smart decisions to set yourself up for happiness, confidence, and success.

Why did the chicken join a decision-making class?
To finally figure out whether to cross the road or not!

Chapter 2

Why Is Decision-Making Important?

One of the main reasons decision-making is so important is because it helps you take control of your life.

When you make decisions, you become the captain of your own ship. You get to choose your own path and shape your future. Whether it's selecting your hobbies, picking your friends, or deciding how to spend your time, every choice you make contributes to who you are and what you will become.

Decision-making also helps you solve problems and overcome challenges. Life is full of obstacles, and knowing how to make good decisions can guide you through difficult situations. You can find the best solutions by carefully considering your options and weighing the pros and cons. This skill will help you now and as you grow older and face even bigger challenges.

Another reason decision-making is important is that it teaches responsibility.

When you make choices, you must take responsibility for the consequences that follow. If you procrastinate on your homework, you might become stressed and rushed the next day. But if you make the decision to complete your tasks on time, you'll feel accomplished and prepared. Making good decisions helps you become accountable for your actions and builds character.

Also, decision-making helps you become more confident. When you make choices and see positive outcomes, it boosts your self-esteem. You'll feel proud of yourself for making smart decisions and trusting your judgment. This confidence will empower you to tackle new challenges and take risks, knowing you have the skills to make the best choices.

Decision-making is incredibly important for children your age. It allows you to take control of your life, solve problems, learn responsibility, and build confidence. By developing good decision-making skills now, you are setting yourself up for a positive and rewarding future.

So, remember to think carefully, consider your options, and make choices that always align with your goals and values.

Benefits of Making Smart Choices

Making smart choices is an essential skill that every young person should learn. It helps you navigate through life by making good decisions to achieve your goals. This section will explore the many benefits of making smart choices.

One of the biggest advantages of making smart choices is that it leads to better outcomes. When you take the time to think through your options and consider the consequences, you are more likely to make decisions that will benefit you in the long run. For example, if you have a big project due, choosing to start early and work consistently will result in a higher-quality finished product, reducing stress and ensuring success. You will also get better grades!

Another benefit of making smart choices is increased confidence. When you make good decisions, you feel good about yourself and your abilities. This confidence can carry over into other areas of your life, empowering you to take on new challenges and believe in your own abilities. By trusting your decision-making skills, you become more self-assured and capable of achieving your goals.

Making smart choices also helps you build strong relationships. When you make thoughtful decisions, you consider the impact on others and choose actions that promote harmony and understanding. For example, if your friend is upset, making the choice to listen and offer support instead of ignoring their feelings can strengthen your friendship and create a more positive and supportive environment.

Additionally, making smart choices leads to better problem-solving skills. When you practice decision-making regularly, you become more skilled at analyzing situations, considering different perspectives, and finding creative solutions. These problem-solving skills are valuable in your personal life, school, and future jobs and careers.

Lastly, making smart choices teaches you responsibility and accountability. When you take ownership of your decisions, you learn to accept the consequences, whether they are positive or negative. This mindset helps you grow and learn from your mistakes, taking responsibility for your actions and making improvements for the future.

Making smart choices is a crucial skill that provides numerous benefits.

It leads to better outcomes, increased confidence, stronger relationships, improved problem-solving skills, and teaches responsibility and accountability.

By honing your decision-making skills, you are equipping yourself with the tools necessary to navigate through life successfully.

Consequences of Poor Decision-Making

We all make decisions every day, big and small. Sometimes, we make good decisions that lead to positive outcomes. But other times, we make poor decisions that can have negative consequences. In this section, we will explore the consequences of poor decision-making and learn why it is important to make smart choices.

One consequence of poor decision-making is that it can lead to unfavorable outcomes. For example, if you decide to procrastinate on studying for a test, the consequence may be that you don't do well and receive a low grade. Similarly, if you decide to eat junk food instead of a healthy meal, you may feel tired and sluggish afterward.

Another consequence of poor decision-making is that it can harm relationships. Making decisions without considering how they might affect others can lead to hurt feelings and misunderstandings. For instance, if you choose to exclude a friend from a game, they may feel left out and upset. Making thoughtless decisions can strain friendships and cause unnecessary conflicts.

Poor decision-making can also have long-term consequences. Sometimes, the effects of our choices can last for a long time. For instance, if you decide to skip brushing your teeth every day, the consequence may be cavities and tooth decay in the future. It's important to consider the long-term effects of your decisions to avoid potential harm or regret down the road.

Lastly, poor decision-making can affect our self-confidence and self-esteem. When we consistently make choices that have negative consequences, it can make us doubt our abilities and judgment. However, by learning from these mistakes and making better decisions in the future, we can rebuild our confidence and improve our decision-making skills.

As you can see, making poor decisions can have several consequences. It can lead to unfavorable outcomes, harm relationships, have long-term negative effects, and impact our self-esteem. However, we can become better decision-makers by understanding the importance of making smart choices and learning from our mistakes.

Remember, every decision you make is an opportunity to learn and grow, so choose wisely! To help you do this, you need to understand how decisions are made.

"Life is a journey, and every decision is a step on that path. Trust yourself, and you'll reach amazing destinations!"
- Anonymous

Chapter 3
The Decision-Making Process

Often in life, we encounter situations where we need to decide. It could be as simple as what to have for lunch or as important as choosing which after-school activity to participate in. Understanding when to decide is the first step in becoming a skilled decision-maker.

Let's explore how to recognize the need for a decision and why it is essential for you to develop good decision-making skills.

Recognizing the need for a decision means understanding that there is a problem or a choice to be made. You might feel stuck or unsure about what to do.

For example, imagine having a free weekend and deciding between going to the cinema with your friends or staying home to finish your homework. Recognizing the need for a decision means realizing that you have conflicting options and must choose one.

Why is recognizing the need for a decision important?

Well, making decisions is a part of life. Our choices can significantly impact our happiness, success, and overall well-being. By recognizing the need for a decision, you are taking control of your life and shaping your future.

It empowers you to consider different possibilities, evaluate the pros and cons, and make choices that align with your values and goals.

As children, it is crucial to develop decision-making skills early on. Making decisions effectively will help you grow into confident and responsible adults. It allows you to express your preferences, make your own choices, and learn from the outcomes.

Also, excellent decision-making skills will benefit you in school, friendships, and other activities. These skills will help you solve problems, think critically, and become independent.

In the upcoming chapters, we will explore different decision-making techniques and tools to help you make smarter choices. Remember, recognizing the need for a decision is the first step towards becoming a skilled decision-maker.

So, next time you find yourself in a situation where you must choose, take a moment to acknowledge the need for a decision.

Embrace the opportunity for learning and growth through the power of decision-making!

Let's begin by getting to know the core steps of the decision-making process. Later in the book, we will discuss a few more to elevate your decision-making skills.

1. Identify the Decision

2. Gather Information

3. Evaluate Your Options

4. Making Your Choice

5. Take Action

Identify the Decision

The first step in making a good decision is to identify what the decision is all about. This means understanding what problem or choice you are facing.

To identify a decision, you need to ask yourself some important questions. What is the problem you need to solve or the choice you have to make? Is it about what to wear to a party or which after-school activity to choose? It could be about how to spend your pocket money or what book to read next.

Whatever it is, identifying the decision is the key to finding an answer or solution.

One helpful technique is to write down the decision you need to make. Use clear and straightforward language so that you can understand it easily. For example, if the decision is about which sport to join, you could write, "Which sport should I choose for my after-school activity?"

Once you have identified the decision, it's time to consider the options available. Remember, there's never just one right answer!

Brainstorm all the possible choices and write them down. You could try out soccer, basketball, tennis or even swimming. The more options you consider, the better your chance of finding the best solution.

Now that you have identified the decision and listed your options, it's time to consider the consequences. What might happen if you choose one option over another? Will it make you happy, help you learn something new, or improve your skills?

It's a good idea always to consider both the advantages and disadvantages of each choice to make an informed decision.

Remember, making decisions can be fun and exciting! By identifying the decision, brainstorming options, and thinking about the consequences, you are well on your way to becoming a decision-making pro.

Identifying Available Options

When making decisions, it's crucial to have all the information at hand. One of the first steps in the decision-making process is to identify your options. This will help you evaluate and choose your best course of action.

Let's dive into how you can identify your options effectively!

Brainstorming

One great way to identify options is by brainstorming. Get some paper and a pencil, and write down all the possible choices you can think of, even if they may seem far-fetched or impossible at this time. Remember, no idea is too big or small! Thinking about different ways you could solve the problem or approach the decision is brainstorming.

Ask For Help

Sometimes, thinking of all the options yourself can be challenging, and that's okay! Don't hesitate to ask for help from your family, friends, or teachers. They may have different perspectives and ideas that you still need to consider.

Research

Another helpful way to identify options is by doing some research. Look for information online, in books, or even by talking to experts related to your decision. The more you know, the more options you'll have.

Consider Consequences

While brainstorming and researching, it's crucial to consider each option's potential consequences. Some choices may have positive outcomes, while others may have negative effects. Understanding the possible results will help you weigh the options and make a smarter decision.

Prioritize

Once you have a list of options, it's time to prioritize them. Think about which choices align with your values, interests, and goals. Consider the pros and cons of your options and compare them to find the best fit.

Remember, identifying options is just one step in making a decision. It's essential to keep an open mind and be willing to explore various possibilities. Sometimes, there may be less obvious options.

You'll be equipped to make a well-informed decision by identifying all the available options. So, grab a pen and paper, ask for help when needed, conduct research, and consider the consequences.

In the next chapter, we will look at different ways you could use to gather the information you need to ensure you have all the facts before making your decision.

***

Why did the teddy bear spend so long picking a bedtime story?
It couldn't "bear" to make a decision and wanted to hear them all!

Chapter 4

Gather Information

Now that you understand the importance of making smart choices, we can move on to the next step, gathering information. This step is crucial in helping you make the best decisions possible.

So, let's get to it!

Collecting as much information as possible is essential when faced with a decision. Knowledge is like a puzzle; the more pieces you have, the clearer the picture becomes. Here are some tips to help you gather the right information:

Identify What You Need to Know

Start by figuring out what you need to learn about the situation. What facts are missing? What are the possible outcomes? Identifying your information gaps will guide you in your search.

Ask Questions

Curiosity is your superpower! Ask questions to understand the problem better. Whether talking to trusted adults, researching, or observing the situation, the more you explore, the more knowledge you gain.

Use Reliable Sources

In the internet age, it's vital to use trustworthy sources of information. Look for books, articles, or websites from experts or reliable organizations. Remember, only some things you find online may be accurate, so double-check your sources!

Consider Different Perspectives

Gather information from different viewpoints. Talk to people who have experienced similar situations or have different opinions. This will help you see the bigger picture and make a well-rounded decision.

Organize Your Findings

Keep track of the information you gather. You can create a list, draw a mind map, or even use a digital tool to organize your thoughts. This way, you will remember all the crucial details while deciding.

Analyze the Information

Now that you have collected all the necessary information, it's time to analyze it. Look for patterns, similarities, or differences. Consider the pros and cons of each option before moving forward.

Gathering information is like building a solid foundation for your decision-making process. The more information you gather, the more confident and informed your choices will be.

So, young decision-makers, embrace your curiosity and embark on an exciting quest for knowledge. Use your questioning skills, seek reliable sources, and consider different perspectives. Gathering information makes you one step closer to becoming a master decision-maker!

Researching and Gathering Facts

As previously mentioned, making smart choices involves gathering information and facts to help you make informed decisions. When faced with a decision, it's important to take the time to gather the necessary information before making up your mind. This section will explore the importance of researching and gathering facts in more detail before deciding.

Researching is like being a detective. It involves asking questions, finding answers, and gathering information from various sources. One way to gather facts is by using the internet. Many reliable websites and online resources can provide valuable information about different topics. However, using trusted sources and verifying the information is important to ensure its accuracy.

Another way to gather facts is by visiting the library. Libraries have a vast collection of books, magazines, and newspapers to help you learn about different subjects. Librarians are also there to assist you in finding the right resources and guiding you through the research process.

Talking to experts is another excellent way to gather facts. Experts have specialized knowledge and can provide valuable insights to help you make better decisions. For example, if you're considering getting a pet, talking to a veterinarian can give you important information about different types of animals and their needs.

In addition to gathering facts, it's also essential to consider different perspectives. People may have different opinions and experiences that can influence their decisions. By listening to others and considering their thoughts, you can better understand the situation and make a more balanced decision.

Remember, making informed decisions is about gathering as much information as possible, considering different viewpoints, and using critical thinking skills. It's okay to take your time to research before making a decision. The more facts you gather, the better equipped you will be to make smart choices.

Seeking Advice From Trusted Sources

Making decisions can be tricky, especially when you have so many options. But don't worry!

In this section, we will learn the importance of seeking advice from trusted sources when making decisions.

Sometimes, it can be overwhelming to make decisions on our own.

That's where seeking advice from trusted sources comes in handy. Trusted sources are people who have experience, knowledge, and expertise in the area you need help with. It could be your parents, teachers, or even friends who have faced similar situations.

So, why is seeking advice important?

Well, trusted sources can provide us with different perspectives and valuable insights. They can help us consider things we might have overlooked to help us make more informed decisions.

When seeking advice, choosing the right people to ask is crucial. You always want to find someone who has your best interests at heart and who will give you honest and objective advice.

Sometimes our friends might not be the best people to ask because they might be biased or need more knowledge about the situation.

It's important to understand that only some people's advice will be right for you, so it's essential to consider multiple perspectives.

Here are some tips to help you make the most out of seeking advice:

Identify the problem

You need to clearly understand what decision you need to make and what information you need. Only by being sure of what you're deciding about will you be able to make the appropriate decision.

Choose Trusted Sources

Please seek advice from people you trust who have experience or knowledge in the area you need help with, as their expertise will provide you with valuable insight.

Listen Carefully

When seeking advice, actively listen to what the person is saying. Take notes if needed, and ask questions to clarify any doubts.

Consider Multiple Perspectives

Don't rely on just one person's advice. Seek out different opinions and weigh the pros and cons of each.

Be Open-Minded

Being open-minded means being willing to consider and accept new ideas and opinions. It's like having a door in your mind that's always open to learning and understanding. When you are open-minded, you listen to others without judging them. This doesn't mean you have to agree with what you are told.

Make Your Own Decision

It's important to remember that the final decision is yours to make. Use the advice you received as guidance, but ultimately, trust your instincts.

Seeking advice from trusted sources is a valuable skill to help you become a better decision-maker. Feel free to reach out for help when you need it. Remember, making decisions is a part of growing up; with practice, you will become more confident in your choices.

In the next chapter, we will discuss evaluating the information you gather to make the best possible choice.

***

> *"It's okay to be afraid of making the wrong choice, but it's not okay to let fear stop you from deciding."*
> *- Anonymous*

Chapter 5
Evaluate Your Options

Now that you have identified your goal and brainstormed some fantastic options, it's time to evaluate them. Evaluating options means considering each choice's pros and cons and considering which is the best fit for you.

Sometimes this can feel overwhelming, so here are some tips to help you evaluate your options like a star.

Make a List

Write down all the options you came up with while gathering information. Seeing them on paper will help you visualize and compare them better. This will also ensure that everything is remembered and noticed.

Think About the Benefits

Consider the positive outcomes or benefits of each option. Will it make you feel good? Will it help you reach your goal? Take note of the benefits of each choice.

Consider the Drawbacks

Now, let's think about each option's potential downsides or drawbacks. Will it take a lot of time? Will it cost a lot of money? Will it make you feel guilty? Write down any concerns or disadvantages for each choice.

Weigh the Pros and Cons

Take a moment to reflect on each option's benefits and drawbacks. Which ones are more important to you? Are there any options that have more pros than cons? Circle or highlight the possibilities that seem most promising. Assign a value or weight to each pro and con based on how significant it is for you. This will help you prioritize and make a more balanced decision.

Ask for Advice

It's always helpful to get a second opinion! Talk to your parents, teachers, or friends about your options. They might offer valuable insights or share their experiences that can guide you in making a smart choice.

Trust Your Gut

Remember, you know yourself best. Sometimes, your intuition can be a great guide. If an option feels right to you, even if it doesn't have the most pros or the fewest cons, consider giving it some extra thought.

You are taking an important step toward making a smart choice by evaluating your options. Remember, there is no right or wrong answer. By carefully considering the pros and cons, you can make the decision that feels right for you and helps you reach your goal.

In the next section, you will learn how to decide.

Weighing the Pros and Cons

When faced with a decision, it's essential to consider the advantages and disadvantages of each option.

These advantages are called 'pros,' and the disadvantages are called 'cons.' We can make informed choices that align with our values and desires by carefully thinking about the pros and cons.

The Benefits of Weighing the Pros and Cons

Clear Thinking

By listing out the pros and cons, we can visualize the different aspects of each option. It helps us to organize our thoughts and make clear, rational decisions.

Avoiding Regrets

Weighing the pros and cons allows us to anticipate the consequences of our choices. It helps us avoid impulsive decisions that we might regret later.

Understanding Priorities

We can identify what is most important to us by considering the pros and cons. It helps us prioritize our values and make decisions that align with our long-term goals.

Building Confidence

When we make decisions based on careful consideration, we feel more confident about our choices. We become responsible for our decisions and take ownership of the outcomes.

Weighing the pros and cons is a valuable decision-making tool that helps us consider the potential outcomes of our choices. By understanding the benefits and following the tips mentioned in this chapter, you can make smarter decisions that lead to a happier and more fulfilling life. Remember, practice makes perfect, so keep honing your decision-making skills, and you'll become a star in no time!

Considering the Potential Outcomes

As you know, some decisions can have a bigger impact on your life. That's why it's important to take the time to think about the potential outcomes before making a decision.

When we talk about potential outcomes, we mean the different results or consequences that could result from our choices. It's like looking into a crystal ball and imagining what might happen if we choose one path over another. Considering these potential outcomes, we can make smarter choices and feel more confident about our decisions.

So, how can we do this?

Before making a decision, it's important to learn as much as possible about the options available. For example, if you're considering joining a sports team, find out what sports are available, how much time it will require, and what skills you need.

This information will help you understand the potential outcomes of your decision.

Next, think about the short-term and long-term consequences of each option. Short-term consequences will happen right away, while long-term consequences could happen in the future.

For example, if you spend all your allowance on toys now, the short-term consequence is that you'll have fun playing with them.

But the long-term consequence might be that you will need more money to save for something special later.

It's also important to consider how your decision might affect others. Will it make them happy, upset, or indifferent? Thinking about the potential outcomes for everyone involved can help you make a more thoughtful decision.

Lastly, remember to trust your gut intuition. Sometimes, deep down, we have a feeling about what the best decision is. If you have a strong feeling about something, it's worth paying attention to. Trusting your gut or listening to the little voice inside you is a skill that will benefit you throughout your life in all sorts of situations.

Considering the potential outcomes is an essential part of making smart choices. Once you've done this, you'll be fully prepared to make your decision.

Why did the crayon refuse to make a decision?
It was afraid it would "color" outside the lines of its comfort zone!

Chapter 6

Making Your Choice

Visualizing different outcomes can be a helpful step in making your choice. Take a moment to imagine what might happen with each option and how you would feel in those situations.

Close your eyes and picture yourself in different scenarios. Think about the happiness, excitement, or satisfaction you might experience with one choice and compare it to how you might feel with another. This can give you a clearer understanding of which option aligns better with your emotions and goals.

Consider the feelings that arise when you think about each outcome. Does one option make you feel more confident and content, while another makes you feel uneasy or stressed? Trusting your emotions and understanding how each choice impacts your feelings can provide valuable insights into what's right for you.

Remember, your feelings are essential guides in decision-making. While facts and logic are important, it's also crucial to acknowledge and respect your emotions. The choice that resonates positively with your heart and mind is likely the one that will lead to a more fulfilling and satisfying outcome.

Always take the time to visualize and feel each potential outcome, and let your emotions guide you toward the right and best decision for you.

The more decisions you make, the better you'll become at making smart choices. So keep exploring, learning, and making decisions that will help you become the best version of yourself.

Trusting Your Instincts

When it comes to making decisions, it can sometimes feel overwhelming. You might find yourself asking, "How do I know what is the right choice?" Well, that's where your instincts come in! Your instincts are like your inner voice, guiding you toward what feels right or wrong. Trusting your instincts is an important skill that can help you make smart choices in life.

So, what exactly are instincts?

Instincts are your natural feelings and reactions to different situations. They are like a built-in alarm system that helps you navigate through life. For example, have you ever met someone new and instantly felt comfortable or uncomfortable around them?

That is your instincts at work, trying to tell you something important.

Trusting your instincts means paying attention to those feelings and listening to what they are trying to tell you.

Sometimes, your instincts might tell you that a specific decision is not the best for you. Maybe you get a funny feeling in your tummy, or your heart starts beating faster. These are signals that something might be off, and listening to them is important.

On the other hand, your instincts can also guide you toward making great choices. Have you ever felt that something wonderful was about to happen? Maybe you felt excited or happy without really knowing why. These positive instincts can lead you to incredible opportunities and experiences.

Trusting your instincts is not always easy, especially when others have different opinions or you are unsure of what to do. But remember, you are the expert on your own feelings and experiences. No one knows you better than you know yourself!

To better trust your instincts, take some time to pause and listen to what your body and mind are telling you. Pay attention to that little voice inside your head that says, "Go for it!" or "Be careful." Take a deep breath, trust yourself, and confidently decide.

Remember, trusting your instincts is a skill that gets better with practice. The more you listen to your inner voice, the more it will guide you toward making smart choices. So, trust yourself, believe in your instincts, and let them guide you on this exciting decision-making journey!

Using Critical Thinking Skills

Critical thinking is an essential skill that helps us make smart choices in life. It involves using our brainpower to analyze, evaluate, and solve problems. When we use critical thinking skills, we become better decision-makers to make choices that will benefit us in the long run.

One way to use critical thinking skills is by asking questions.

When faced with a decision, we should ask ourselves: What are my options? What are the pros and cons of each option? What are the possible consequences of each choice? We can gather information and think about the best course of action by asking these questions.

Another important aspect of critical thinking is considering different perspectives.

Sometimes, we may think our way is the only right way, but that's not always the case. We can better understand the situation by considering different viewpoints to make more informed decisions. We can talk to our friends, family, or teachers to get their opinions and listen to their ideas.

Critical thinking also involves evaluating the reliability of information.

In today's digital age, we are bombarded with information from various sources. It's essential to think critically and question the accuracy and credibility of the information we come across. We can fact-check, look for evidence, and seek expert opinions to ensure we have reliable information to base our decisions on.

Lastly, critical thinking requires us to think ahead and anticipate the consequences of our choices.

We should not only consider the immediate benefits but also the long-term effects. Will this choice help me to achieve my goals? Will it make me happy in the future? We can make choices that align with our values and aspirations by thinking ahead.

Using critical thinking skills is crucial for making smart choices. We can become better decision-makers by asking questions, considering different perspectives, evaluating information, and thinking ahead.

Before taking action when faced with your next decision, remember to use your critical thinking skills and make choices that will lead you to success and happiness.

***

*"In life, you have to make many decisions.
Choose wisely, and trust that even if it doesn't turn out
as planned, you'll learn and grow from it."*
- Anonymous

Chapter 7

Take Action

Once you have completed all the previous steps, it's time to take action and finally put your decision into motion. This is where all your hard work pays off, and you start to see the results of your smart choices.

Taking action means doing something to make your decision happen. Let's say you decided to start a club at school. Now it's time to gather your friends, find a meeting place, and set a date for your first meeting. Taking action also involves overcoming any obstacles that may come your way. You may need permission from your teacher or principal to start the club or figure out how to raise funds for supplies.

Whatever challenges you face, believe you have the skills to handle them.

One important thing to remember when taking action is to stay positive and focused. It's normal to feel nervous or unsure about what will happen next, but remember that you have already done the hard work of making a smart choice. Trust yourself and believe in your decision. If you encounter obstacles or setbacks, don't give up. Stay determined and keep pushing forward.

Taking action also means being responsible for your decision. For example, if you decide to join a sports team, it's important to show up to practice on time, listen to your coach, and put in your best effort. By taking responsibility for your decision, you respect yourself and others who are counting on you.

Finally, taking action is about learning and growing. Sometimes things don't go exactly as planned, and that's okay. View mistakes and failures as opportunities to learn and improve. Reflect on what went wrong and think about how you can do things differently next time. Remember, making smart choices is a skill that takes practice, and each decision you make is a chance to become better at it.

So, go ahead and take action! Put your decision into motion, overcome obstacles, stay positive and responsible, and always be ready to learn and grow. You have the power to make extraordinary things happen with your smart choices.

Implementing Your Decision

You have just made a smart decision using the skills you have learned in this book. Of course, making your decision is excellent, but as stated above, your choice is only meaningful if you act on it.

Now it's time to put your decision into action. This section will guide you through the process of implementing your decision effectively.

Create a Plan

Start by outlining a plan of action. Break down your decision into smaller steps, and think about what you must do to achieve your goal. Write down each step and make a timeline to keep yourself organized.

Gather Resources

Think about what resources you need to carry out your plan. It could be materials, information, or even support from others. Please make a list of everything you need and find ways to obtain them.

Take Action

It's time to start taking action! Begin with the first step of your plan and work through each task. Remember, even small steps count. Stay focused and motivated, and always ask for help if needed.

Overcome Obstacles

Along the way, you might encounter obstacles that challenge your progress. It's important to be prepared for setbacks and find ways to overcome them. Stay persistent and flexible, and don't give up easily. Always remember every problem has a solution.

Evaluate and Adjust

As you implement your decision, you must evaluate your progress regularly. Ask yourself if you are moving closer to your goal or whether any adjustments are needed. Be honest with yourself and make changes if necessary. Remember, modifying your plan is okay if it leads to a better outcome.

Celebrate Your Success

Once you have successfully implemented your decision, take a moment to celebrate your achievement. You have shown excellent decision-making skills, and it's important to acknowledge your efforts. Treat yourself to something you enjoy or share your success with your family and friends.

Remember, implementing your decision is an essential part of the decision-making process. These steps will turn your decisions into actions to help you achieve your goals. Keep practicing these skills, and you will become a master decision-maker in no time!

Dealing With Possible Challenges

Life is full of surprises, and sometimes we encounter challenges that require us to make tough decisions. Don't worry, though! In section, we will explore how to handle these obstacles and make smart choices even when things get tough.

Identify the Challenge

The first step in dealing with challenges is recognizing and understanding the problem. Please take a moment to think about what is causing the difficulty and try to break it down into smaller parts. By doing this, you can better understand the challenge and find a way to overcome it.

Stay Positive

Challenges can be intimidating, but it's important to maintain a positive mindset. Remember, every obstacle presents an opportunity to learn and grow. Believe in yourself and your ability to find a solution. Positive thinking can help you face challenges with confidence.

Seek Help and Support

Don't be afraid to ask for help! Discuss any issues with a trusted adult, such as a teacher or parent, for guidance and support. They may have experienced similar challenges and be able to offer valuable advice. Asking for help shows strength, not weakness.

Explore Possible Solutions

Once you understand the challenge and have sought help, brainstorm different solutions. Consider the pros and cons of all your options. Think about how they align with your goals and values, and remember, there is often more than one way to solve a problem!

Take Action

After carefully considering your options, it's time to decide and act. Be brave and trust your instincts. Remember, no decision is perfect, but what matters is that you approach it with thoughtfulness and confidence.

Learn from Setbacks

Sometimes, despite our best efforts, things go differently than planned. If you encounter setbacks or make a wrong decision, don't be too hard on yourself. Mistakes are part of life, and they provide valuable lessons. Reflect on what went wrong, learn from it, and use that knowledge to make better choices in the future.

By following these steps, you can develop strong decision-making skills and tackle any challenge that comes your way. Remember, challenges are opportunities in disguise! Embrace them, learn from them, and let them shape you into a resilient and confident individual.

Why did the pencil go to therapy?
It couldn't make up its mind and needed help with "lead"-ing a more decisive life!

Chapter 8

Sitting on the Fence

Imagine finding yourself in a puzzling dilemma, where each choice seems equally appealing or challenging, leaving you hesitant and unsure. This is known as sitting on the fence, where decision-making becomes challenging. In this chapter, we will explore the complexities of indecision and the importance of addressing this in life.

You might find yourself unable to make a decision for various reasons. One common factor is fear of making the wrong choice. The fear of failure or disappointing others can lead to indecision as you hesitate to take action. Additionally, a lack of information or uncertainty about the potential outcomes can leave you feeling stuck and unable to commit to a specific choice.

Sometimes feeling overwhelmed by the complexity of the decision can be another reason for indecisiveness. When faced with multiple options or difficult situations, the importance of the choices ahead may paralyze you, making it difficult to move forward.

Emotional factors, such as conflicting desires or attachments to specific outcomes, can also contribute to hesitation as you grapple with your feelings and find prioritizing one option challenging. It's essential to recognize these reasons for indecision and address them to develop the confidence and clarity needed to make thoughtful and decisive choices.

Understanding Indecision

Indecision can feel like a tug-of-war between two powerful forces, each pulling you in opposite directions. You might be torn between two options, each presenting merits or complications.

Sometimes the fear of making the wrong choice can leave you stuck in a state of analysis paralysis, unable to move forward. Understanding this struggle is the first step in addressing indecision and gaining the clarity needed to make confident decisions.

Root Causes of Hesitation

To overcome indecision, it's crucial to identify the root causes that keep you perched on the fence. Is it the fear of failure that holds you back? Or it's the pressure of external expectations, making you second-guess your choices. You may be worried about missing out on something better.

By acknowledging these obstacles, you can confront and address them head-on. This self-awareness empowers you to break free from hesitation and make choices that align with your values and aspirations.

The Consequences of Inaction

While it may seem safer to avoid making a decision, inaction comes with its price. Procrastination can lead to missed opportunities and delays in progress.

By remaining on the fence, you risk standing still while life passes you by. Understanding the potential consequences of staying in a state of indecision can be a powerful motivator to take action and step confidently into the future.

Gaining Clarity

Gaining clarity about your values, goals, and priorities is an essential step in making confident decisions. Through self-reflection, you can understand what truly matters to you.

By defining your priorities, you can better evaluate options and choose paths that resonate with your authentic self. This clarity becomes your compass, guiding you towards choices that align with your true purpose.

Balancing Logic and Intuition

Confident decision-making involves striking a balance between rational analysis and trusting your intuition. Considering the facts, weighing the pros and cons, and logically assessing the potential outcomes is essential.

However, it's equally crucial to listen to your gut feelings. Intuition often holds valuable insights that logic alone may overlook.

Learning to trust your instincts is a skill that can lead to more confident and aligned decision-making.

Taking the Leap

At some point, you must make a choice and commit to it. Embrace the courage to step off the fence and take action. Understand that every decision is an opportunity for growth and learning.

There are no guarantees of a perfect outcome, but having the courage to decide empowers you to take charge of your life and shape your future.

Embracing the Journey

Regardless of the outcome, each decision contributes to your personal growth and development.

Embrace the journey and its lessons, whether through successes or setbacks. Viewing outcomes as learning experiences fosters a growth mindset, helping you approach future decisions with resilience and a positive attitude. When you understand this, you won't be afraid of making mistakes.

Seeking Support

Don't hesitate to seek support and guidance from trusted friends, family, or mentors. Discussing your options with others can provide valuable perspectives and insights that shed light on your decision. Having a support network helps you navigate challenges with greater confidence and reassurance.

Cultivating Confidence

As you become more comfortable making decisions, your confidence will grow. Embrace the empowerment of taking charge of your life and shaping your future through thoughtful choices.

Confidence in decision-making spills over into other aspects of life, enabling you to face challenges with greater self-assurance.

Learning and Growing

Understand that no one is immune from making mistakes. Embrace imperfection as a part of the learning process, and remember that every decision is an opportunity for growth.

The path to becoming a skilled decision-maker can be challenging. You will develop into a more capable and resilient individual through this experience by learning from both successes and failures.

As you navigate the complexities of life, armed with the knowledge gained from this chapter, you can approach sitting on the fence with assurance. Embrace the power of decisive action and trust that each choice is a step toward a brighter and more fulfilling future.

Let go of hesitation, embrace the journey of confident decision-making, and step boldly into the future with the knowledge that you can navigate any crossroad with confidence and wisdom.

"In any moment of decision, the best thing you can do is the right thing. The worst thing you can do is nothing."
— Theodore Roosevelt

Chapter 9

Factors Influencing Decision-Making

This chapter explores various factors that can influence your decision-making process. From emotions and peer pressure to past experiences and personal values, understanding these influences will empower you to make more informed and thoughtful choices.

Personal Values and Beliefs

Understanding and defining our personal values and beliefs is an important part of growing up and making smart choices. Our personal values are the things that we believe are most important in life. They guide our actions and help us make decisions that align with what we think is right and wrong.

One of the first steps in developing our values is to think about what matters most to us. Is it kindness, honesty, fairness, or respect? These are just a few examples, but everyone's personal values will be a little different. Take a moment to think about what you believe in and what makes you feel good about yourself.

Once you have a good idea of your personal values, it's important to remember that your values can change and grow over time. As you learn new things and experience different situations, you may find that some of your values become more important to you, while others may not matter as much.

Our personal beliefs are closely tied to our values. Beliefs are the ideas and opinions we hold to be true. They can be about anything, from what we believe spiritually to what we think is right or wrong. It's important to remember that everyone has different beliefs, and that's okay. Respecting others' beliefs is an important part of being a good decision-maker.

Understanding our personal values and beliefs can help us make better decisions. When faced with a tough choice, we can think about what aligns with our values and what feels right. For example, if honesty is one of your values, you would tell the truth even if it is difficult. We can feel good about our choices by staying true to our values.

Remember, your personal values and beliefs are unique to you. It's important to take the time to think about what matters most to you and why. Understanding your values and beliefs allows you to become a confident decision-maker who stays true to yourself.

Understanding the Importance of Personal Values

In this section, we will explore the significance of personal values and how they play a vital role in decision-making. As children, you are constantly faced with big and small choices that shape your lives. Understanding your personal values can help you make smart decisions that align with who you are and what you believe in.

So, what are personal values?

These are the core beliefs and principles that guide our behavior and actions. They are the things that matter most to us and make us unique individuals. For example, trust, honesty, respect, and fairness are some common personal values.

Why are personal values important? Well, imagine if everyone made decisions without considering their values. There would be chaos and confusion. Personal values act as a compass, directing us towards choices that align with who we are and what we believe is right. They help us stay true to ourselves and make decisions that make us feel good about ourselves.

Knowing your personal values can also help you prioritize and make better decisions. You can choose between going to a friend's party or staying home to study for an important test. If your personal value is education, you might prioritize studying because it aligns with your values. On the other hand, if your personal value is friendship, you might choose to go to the party because spending time with friends is important to you.

Understanding your personal values can also help you navigate peer pressure. Sometimes, your friends or classmates may try to influence your decisions. Knowing your values can give you the confidence to stand up for what you believe in and make true choices.

To figure out your personal values, take some time to reflect on what truly matters to you. What qualities do you admire in others? What makes you feel proud or happy? These questions can help you identify your personal values.

Remember, your values are unique to you, and it's okay if they differ from others. Embrace your values and let them guide you as you make smart choices.

Exploring How Beliefs Can Impact Decisions

In our journey of learning decision-making skills, we have already covered the importance of gathering information and considering alternatives. But did you know that our beliefs can also have a significant impact on the decisions we make? Let's explore this fascinating topic and how our beliefs shape our choices.

Beliefs are the ideas and thoughts about ourselves, others, and the world around us. They are like the lenses through which we see the world. Our family, friends, and experiences can influence our beliefs and even the media. Sometimes, we may be unaware of these beliefs, but they can still guide our decision-making process.

For example, suppose we believe trying new things is scary and always leads to failure. In that case, we might avoid taking risks and miss out on exciting opportunities. On the other hand, if we believe in our abilities and have a growth mindset, we will be more open to challenges and learn from our mistakes.

Stereotypes and biases can also influence our beliefs. These are preconceived ideas we have about certain people based on their race, age, gender, or other characteristics. Questioning these beliefs and challenging stereotypes is essential because they can lead to unfair judgments and decisions.

To make smart choices, we must examine our beliefs and ask ourselves if they are based on accurate information or just assumptions.

We can do this by seeking different perspectives, asking questions, and being open-minded. Changing our beliefs is okay if we discover new information that challenges our old ideas.

Understanding how beliefs impact our decisions can help us make more informed choices. We can overcome biases and make fair judgments by recognizing and challenging our beliefs. We can also develop empathy and understanding toward others, essential for building positive relationships.

Remember, as you grow older, your beliefs may change as well. So, always be curious, keep questioning, and be open to new ideas. By exploring how beliefs can impact decisions, you are taking an essential step toward becoming a smart decision-maker!

In the next chapter, let's delve deeper into emotions and how they can influence our decision-making process.

Why did the scarecrow become a great decision-maker?
Because he was outstanding in his field!

Chapter 10

Emotions

Emotions are a big part of who we are as human beings. They can make us happy, sad, angry, scared, or excited. Sometimes, our emotions can even affect the decisions we make. This chapter will explore the world of emotions and learn how to use them to make smart choices.

Understanding our emotions is an important step toward making better decisions. It's vital to recognize and acknowledge our feelings.

For example, if you're feeling angry or frustrated, take a moment to understand why you're feeling that way. Maybe someone said something hurtful, or you didn't get your way. Once you understand your emotions, it becomes easier to deal with them.

Emotions are powerful and can sometimes cloud our judgment.

When we're happy or excited, we might make impulsive decisions without considering the consequences. On the other hand, when we're sad or scared, we might avoid making any decisions at all. Finding a balance and not letting our emotions control us is important.

One technique that can help us manage our emotions is "STOP and THINK." When you find yourself in a situation where your emotions are running high, take a moment to stop and think before you make a decision.

Ask yourself, "Is this the best choice for me right now? How will this decision affect me and others?" If you're feeling emotional, taking a break can help you make a more thoughtful and rational decision later.

Another helpful strategy is to talk to someone you trust about your emotions. It could be a parent, a teacher, or a friend. Sharing your feelings with others can provide a fresh perspective and help you see things more clearly.

Remember, it's okay to feel different emotions. Emotions are a natural part of being human.

The key is not to let them control you but to use them as a guide in making smart choices. You can become a better decision-maker by understanding your emotions, pausing, and seeking guidance from trusted individuals.

So, the next time you decide, remember to tune in to your emotions. They can be your allies in making smart choices.

Let's find out more!

How Emotions Can Affect Decision-Making

Have you ever wondered why sometimes you make decisions that you later regret? Well, one important factor that can influence our decision-making process is our emotions.

Emotions are the feelings we experience in response to different situations, and they can significantly impact our choices.

Sometimes, when we feel happy or excited, we may make impulsive decisions without considering the consequences. For example, buying a toy without considering if it's the best use of our money.

On the other hand, when we are sad or angry, we may make decisions based on those negative emotions, leading to poor choices. For instance, saying hurtful things to a friend during an argument.

Understanding how emotions affect decision-making is important because it helps us make better choices. Here are a few ways emotions can influence our decision-making process:

Fear

When we are scared, our decisions may be driven by a desire to avoid what we fear. This can sometimes prevent us from taking risks or trying new things, even if they could be beneficial in the long run. We are not discussing dangerous risks but doing things that are sometimes out of your comfort zone. Sometimes doing things that are out of our comfort zone leads us to new opportunities.

Excitement

Feeling excited can make us more likely to take risks without considering the consequences. It's important to take a step back and think through our decisions, even when feeling thrilled about something.

Anger

Making decisions when we are angry can lead to impulsive and potentially harmful choices. It's important to calm down and think rationally before acting on our anger.

Happiness

While being happy is wonderful, it can sometimes cloud our judgment and make us overlook potential problems or risks. It's important to balance our happiness with careful consideration of the facts.

We can make smarter choices by being aware of our emotions and how they can affect our decision-making. The next time you are faced with a decision, take a moment to reflect on how you are feeling and consider if your emotions are influencing your choice. Remember, it's always a good idea to take a deep breath, think things through, and decide based on what's best for you and those around you.

Strategies for Managing Emotions

When making decisions, it's important to remember that our emotions can sometimes get in the way. Feelings like fear, excitement, or even anger can cloud our judgment and lead to making poor choices. That's why learning to manage our emotions during decision-making is a valuable skill. Here are some strategies to help you make smart choices while keeping your emotions in check:

Take a Deep Breath

When faced with a tough decision, it's normal to feel overwhelmed. Before making any hasty decisions, take a deep breath and try to calm yourself down. This will allow you to think more clearly and avoid impulsive choices.

Identify Your Emotions

Understanding how you're feeling is the first step in managing your emotions. Take a moment to recognize what emotions are influencing your decision-making process. Are you feeling scared, excited, or frustrated? Acknowledging your feelings will help you understand how they might impact your choices.

Give Yourself Time

Rushing to make a decision can sometimes lead to regret. To make sure you never regret your decisions, always take the time to gather information, weigh your options, and think things through. Giving yourself space and time can help you make a more rational choice than being driven solely by your emotions.

Consider the Consequences

Emotions can sometimes blind us to the potential outcomes of our decisions. Before making a choice, think about the consequences and how they might affect you and others. This will help you make a more informed decision that considers the long-term effects.

Seek Advice

Be bold and ask for help or advice from trusted adults or friends. They can provide a different perspective and help you see things more clearly. Sometimes, an outside opinion can help you manage your emotions and make better decisions.

Managing your emotions during decision-making is a lifelong skill that will serve you well. You'll become a smart decision-maker by taking a step back, recognizing your emotions, and considering the consequences.

So, the next time you're faced with a tough choice, take a moment to manage your emotions to ensure you make the best decision possible.

Sometimes you may feel pressured to make a decision you're uncomfortable with, known as peer pressure. The next chapter will explore how this can affect your decision-making.

***

*"You have brains in your head. You have feet in your shoes.
You can steer yourself any direction you choose."*
- Dr. Seuss

Chapter 11

Peer Pressure

Peer pressure is something that all kids experience at some point in their lives.

It is the feeling of being influenced by our friends or classmates to do something we might not want, which can be both positive or negative, depending on the situation. In this chapter, we will explore what peer pressure is, how it can affect our decisions, and, most importantly, how we can make smart choices even when faced with peer pressure.

Firstly, it is crucial to understand that peer pressure is a natural part of growing up. We all want to fit in and be accepted by our peers, which can sometimes lead us to make choices that we are not comfortable with.

For example, if all our friends are playing a game we don't enjoy, we might still join in to feel included. However, it is essential to remember that we have the power to make our own decisions and should never feel pressured into doing something we don't want to do.

Peer pressure can also be damaging when it involves activities that are harmful or against our values. Standing up for ourselves and our beliefs is crucial, even if it means going against the crowd.

Making smart choices means being confident in our decisions and not succumbing to the pressure to conform.

One way to resist negative peer pressure is to surround ourselves with friends who support and respect our choices.

True friends will not try to force us into doing things we don't want to do. Building a network of positive influences encouraging us to make smart decisions is essential.

Another strategy is to think about the consequences of our actions.

We should ask ourselves whether the choice we are about to make aligns with our values and long-term goals. Sometimes, taking a step back and evaluating the situation can help us make better decisions, even under pressure.

Recognizing Different Types of Peer Pressure

In our journey through life, we often find ourselves influenced by the people around us. One powerful influence that we all experience is peer pressure. Peer pressure can be defined as our friend's or peers' influence on us to behave in a certain way or make specific choices.

It is important to understand that not all peer pressure is negative, so you should be aware of different types of peer pressure so that you can recognize and understand it..

Positive Peer Pressure

Positive peer pressure occurs when our friends encourage us to make good choices and do the right thing. For example, suppose a friend encourages us to study hard for an upcoming test or join a community service project. In that case, it can be considered positive peer pressure. Surrounding ourselves with friends who have a positive influence can help us become better individuals and make smarter decisions.

Negative Peer Pressure

On the other hand, negative peer pressure happens when our friends push us to do things we know are wrong or make choices that could harm us. This can include engaging in risky behaviors like smoking, drinking alcohol, or skipping school.

Negative peer pressure can be challenging to resist. Still, it is essential to understand that we have the power to say no and make decisions that align with our values and well-being.

Indirect Peer Pressure

Another type of peer pressure is indirect peer pressure. This happens when we observe others engaging in certain behaviors, and we feel pressured to do the same.

For instance, if we see our friends buying the latest gadgets or wearing trendy clothes, we might feel compelled to do the same, even if it means going against our better judgment. Indirect peer pressure can influence our decision-making skills, and it is crucial to recognize it and make choices that are right for us, not just to fit in.

Self-Imposed Peer Pressure

Sometimes, we pressure ourselves to conform to certain expectations, even if our friends aren't directly influencing us. This is called self-imposed peer pressure.

For instance, if we need to excel in every subject because we think our friends expect it, we are putting unnecessary pressure on ourselves. It is important to remember that we should set our own goals and make choices that make us happy rather than seeking approval from others.

By recognizing and understanding the different types of peer pressure, we can become more aware of its influence on our decision-making skills.

Remember, being true to ourselves is okay, even if it means going against the crowd. Making smart choices that align with our values and well-being is the key to a fulfilling and successful life.

Strategies for Resisting Negative Peer Pressure

This section will discuss practical strategies to help you resist negative peer pressure and make smart choices.

Peer pressure is a common experience during childhood and adolescence, but it is essential to stand up for yourself and make decisions that align with your values and beliefs.

Know Yourself

The first step to resisting negative peer pressure is understanding who you are and what you stand for.

Take time to reflect on your values, interests, and goals. This self-awareness will give you a strong foundation to make the right decisions.

Choose Your Friends Wisely

Surround yourself with friends who share similar values and respect your choices. True friends will support you, even if you decide to go against the crowd. Avoid individuals who consistently pressure you into doing things that make you uncomfortable or go against your values.

Practice Saying No

Saying no can be challenging, but it is a crucial skill when faced with negative peer pressure.

Role-play different scenarios with a trusted adult or friend so you feel more confident in saying no when the situation arises. Remember, it's okay to say no and stick to your principles.

Offer Alternatives

If your friends are pressuring you into doing something uncomfortable, suggest alternative activities that align with your values.

For example, if they want to skip school, propose a fun and safe activity they can enjoy without breaking any rules.

Seek Support From Adults

Trusted adults, such as parents, teachers, or mentors, can provide guidance and support when dealing with negative peer pressure. Talk to them about your concerns and seek their advice, as they can help you navigate difficult situations and provide valuable insights.

Trust Your Instincts

Always listen to your gut feeling. It something doesn't feel right, it probably isn't. Trust yourself and your judgment. Don't be afraid to walk away from situations that make you uncomfortable or compromise your values.

Build Self-Confidence

Develop a strong sense of self-confidence through activities that showcase your talents and interests. Participate in clubs, sports, or hobbies that boost your self-esteem. When you believe in yourself, it becomes easier to resist negative peer pressure.

Peer pressure is a part of life, but it doesn't mean we must give in to it.

By understanding the influence of peer pressure, surrounding ourselves with positive friends, and thinking about the consequences of our actions, we can make smart choices even when faced with difficult situations.

Remember, being yourself and standing up for what you believe in is okay. Making decisions that align with your values and goals is the key to being happy and confident in who you are.

Let's now take a look at some decisions you may encounter.

Why did the tomato turn red when faced with a decision?
It was just ripe for making up its mind!

Chapter 12

Types of Decisions You May Encounter

This chapter will explore the art of everyday decision-making to learn valuable skills which will help you make smart choices.

Understanding the importance of decisions is the first step. As you know, every decision you make has big or small consequences. By becoming aware of the impact of your choices, you will start to see the value in making thoughtful decisions.

Remember, even small decisions can sometimes impact your life more than you anticipated.

As you've already learned, it's important to gather information to make smart choices. Before deciding, take the time to collect all the facts and explore your options. Let's say you have to decide what to do after school. You can gather information by asking your friends about their plans, checking out different activities in your community, or even talking to your parents or teachers. The more information you have, the better equipped you will be to make a decision that suits your interests and goals.

Once you have gathered information, it's time to evaluate your options by considering the pros and cons of each choice. Think about how each option aligns with your values, interests, and priorities. For example, joining an after-school art club might be an excellent choice if you have a passion for art. On the other hand, joining a soccer team could be more fitting if you love sports.

You can make decisions that align with your passions and values by evaluating your options.

Finally, it's time to make your decision. Trust your instincts and listen to your gut feeling. Remember, there is no right or wrong decision. What matters is that you have thoughtfully considered your options and made the right choice. And remember, every decision is a learning opportunity. If things don't turn out as expected, reflect on what you've learned and use that knowledge to make even smarter choices in the future.

Choosing What to Wear

Making decisions about what to wear can be both fun and challenging. Our clothes keep us warm, protect us from the weather and help us express our unique personalities and styles.

This section will explore tips and tricks to help you make smart choices when choosing what clothes to wear.

The first thing to consider when selecting an outfit is the weather. Is it hot or cold outside? Is it raining or snowing? Dressing appropriately for the weather will ensure you stay comfortable throughout the day. Choose light and breathable fabrics like cotton or linen if it's hot. On the other hand, if it's cold, opt for warm and cozy clothes such as jackets and sweaters.

Next, think about the occasion or activity you'll be attending. Is it a formal event like a wedding or a casual outing with friends? Different occasions call for different types of outfits. Consider wearing a dress or a suit for formal events. At the same time, casual outings allow for more relaxed clothing like jeans and T-shirts.

Consider your own personal style and what makes you feel confident and comfortable. Do you prefer bright colors or more neutral tones? Are you into trendy fashion, or do you have a unique style? Remember, your clothes should reflect who you are and make you feel good about yourself.

It's also important to consider any dress codes or rules that might be in place. Some schools, for example, have specific uniforms or guidelines on what to wear. Make sure to follow these rules, as they are in place to promote fairness and respect for everyone.

Lastly, don't be afraid to experiment and have fun with your outfits! Fashion is a way to express your creativity and personality. Mix and match different clothing items, try out new accessories, and don't be afraid to be bold and unique.

Remember, choosing what to wear is all about expressing yourself, feeling comfortable, and making smart decisions. By considering the weather, the occasion, your personal style, any dress codes, and having fun with your outfits, you'll be well on your way to becoming a fashion-savvy decision-maker!

Deciding What to Eat for Breakfast

As breakfast is the day's most important meal, it is a good idea to begin your day with something healthy and nutritious. Sometimes, deciding what to eat for breakfast can be confusing. This section will help you choose the best breakfast options for a great start to your day!

When deciding what to eat for breakfast, it's crucial to consider your body's needs. Your body requires proper energy; a healthy breakfast provides that energy. So, think about foods that will give you the energy boost you need to sustain you through your day.

One smart choice is to include a variety of food groups in your breakfast. This means having foods from different categories, such as fruits, grains, dairy, and proteins.

For example, you can have a bowl of whole-grain cereal with low-fat milk topped with fresh berries. This way, you'll get carbohydrates for energy, calcium for strong bones, and vitamins from fruits.

Another helpful tip is to listen to your body. Please pay attention to how different foods make you feel after eating them. For instance, if eating sugary cereals makes you feel tired and sluggish, opting for a healthier alternative, like oatmeal or whole wheat toast with peanut butter, is a good idea.

Planning your breakfast the night before can also make decision-making easier. You can create a menu or list healthy breakfast options and stick it on your fridge. That way, you can select a breakfast item from your list every morning without spending too much time thinking about it.

Always remember portion sizes. Eating the right amount of food to fuel your body without overeating is important. Pay attention to suggested serving sizes on food labels and listen to your body's hunger cues.

Deciding what to eat for breakfast is an important decision affecting your energy levels and overall well-being.

By considering the different food groups, listening to your body, planning ahead, and being mindful of portion sizes, you can make smart choices that will set you up with all the energy you need for the day ahead. Breakfast is the fuel that jump-starts your day, so choose wisely and enjoy a nutritious and delicious morning meal!

School-Related Decisions

Making decisions can sometimes feel overwhelming, especially when it comes to school. But don't worry. This section will help you become a star at making smart choices regarding school-related decisions. Whether choosing a suitable extracurricular activity, deciding on a study schedule, or selecting the best friends to study with, this section will guide you through it all.

One important school-related decision is choosing the right extracurricular activity. Do you enjoy playing sports, painting, or playing a musical instrument? Think about what you're passionate about and what activities make you happy. Consider your strengths and interests, and then talk to your parents or teachers for guidance. Remember, choosing something you enjoy is important, as it will make your school experience more pleasant and memorable.

Another school-related decision is planning your study schedule. Schoolwork can be overwhelming, but you can manage it all with a well-structured study schedule. Start by organizing your time and setting aside specific hours for studying. Find a quiet and comfortable place to work, free from distractions. Break your study time into smaller chunks with short breaks to keep your focus sharp. Remember, being consistent is key, so stick to your schedule and watch your grades improve.

Choosing the right friends to study with is also an important decision. Surrounding yourself with positive and motivated friends can greatly impact your academic success. Look for friends who share similar goals and have a good work ethic. Together, you can motivate and support each other. Remember, it's not all about studying; make sure to have fun and enjoy your time together.

Lastly, you may face decisions related to your future education. You may need to choose between different schools or decide on the subjects you want to focus on. Talk to your parents, teachers, and school counselors to gather information and explore your options. Consider your interests, goals, and what will make you happy. Remember, changing your mind along the way is okay, so be open to considering new opportunities and possibilities.

Making school-related decisions can be tough, but you can make smart choices with the right tools and guidance. Remember to consider your interests, strengths, and goals when deciding about extracurricular activities, study schedules, friends, and future education. By making well-informed choices, you'll set yourself up for success and make the most out of your school experience.

Selecting Extracurricular Activities

Being a child is the perfect time to explore new hobbies and interests. Extracurricular activities are great for fun and learning important life skills. This section will guide you in selecting the right extracurricular activities that suit your interests and help you develop decision-making skills.

Explore Your Interests

The first step in selecting extracurricular activities is to think about what interests you. Do you love sports? Are you passionate about music? Are you curious about science? Take some time to brainstorm and list activities you would like to try.

Consider Your Strengths

While exploring your interests, also think about your strengths. Are you good at problem-solving? Do you enjoy working with others? Identifying your strengths can help you choose activities that align with your abilities and talents.

Research Different Options

Once you have a list of activities, it's time to do some research. Look for clubs, classes, or teams in your community that offer the activities you are interested in. Read about them in books or search online to learn more. Talk to your teachers or friends to get recommendations.

Talk to Your Parents

Share your list of activities with your parents or guardians. They can provide valuable guidance to help you make informed decisions. Discuss your interests and strengths with them and ask for their support in exploring these activities.

Try Before Committing

Before signing up for a long-term commitment, try out different activities. Attend trial classes or practices to get a feel for each activity. This will help you determine whether you enjoy it and if it suits your preferences.

Set Goals

Once you have chosen an activity, set some goals for yourself. Do you want to improve your skills? Make new friends? Have fun?

Setting relevant goals will help you stay motivated and focused on your chosen activity.

Balance Your Schedule

While extracurricular activities are fantastic, it's important to keep yourself manageable. Make sure to balance your schoolwork, family time, and relaxation with your chosen activities. Prioritize and manage your time wisely.

Remember, the most essential part of selecting extracurricular activities is to have fun and learn new things. Trying different activities is okay until you find the ones that genuinely excite you. So go ahead and explore the world of extracurricular activities, make smart choices, and enjoy the journey of discovering your passions!

Determining How to Study Effectively

When it comes to studying, it can sometimes feel confusing. But don't worry. You can become a star student with the right strategies! This section will discuss some practical ways to study and make the most out of your study time.

Find Your Study Style

Every child is unique, and so is their preferred study style. Some kids learn better by reading, while others prefer visual aids or hands-on activities. Experiment with different study techniques to find out what works best for you. It could be creating flashcards, drawing diagrams, or even teaching the material to a stuffed animal!

Create a Study Schedule

Planning is vital to success! Create a study schedule by setting aside specific times for studying and sticking to it. This will help you develop good study habits and ensure enough time for all your subjects. Remember to include short breaks to recharge your brain!

Organize Your Study Area

A cluttered study area can distract you from focusing on your work. Keep your desk tidy, and have all the necessary materials within reach. Getting into the habit of creating a clean study environment will help you stay focused and save time searching for things when needed.

Break It Down

Large tasks can feel overwhelming, so break them into smaller, manageable chunks. If you have a big project or a lot of information to learn, divide it into smaller sections and tackle them one at a time. Celebrate your progress as you complete each section – it will motivate you to keep going!

Use Different Resources

Textbooks are excellent, but don't limit yourself to just one resource. Explore other materials like websites, videos, or educational apps related to your subject. Using different resources can make studying more fun and help you understand the material from different perspectives.

Take Breaks and Reward Yourself

Studying for long periods without a break can lead to burnout. Take short breaks every 20-30 minutes to rest your mind and recharge. Use this time to stretch, have a healthy snack, or even play a quick game. Remember to reward yourself after completing a study session or achieving a goal!

Remember, studying is not just about memorizing facts; it's about understanding and applying what you learn. Following these tips will make you a star at studying effectively and making smart educational choices.

So, the next time you are faced with a decision, whether choosing what to eat for breakfast or deciding how to spend your free time, remember these steps: gather information, evaluate your options, and trust your instincts. By practicing these decision-making skills, you can make smart choices that will positively shape your life.

***

"When you have to make a choice and don't make it, that, in itself, is a choice."
- William James

Chapter 13

Making Smart Decisions About Spending

Spending decisions are critical and the earlier you learn how to make smart money decisions, the better off you will be. So, let's get into that.

This chapter explores the essential aspects of making wise decisions about spending money. Money is a valuable resource, and learning how to use it responsibly is an important life skill.

By understanding how and when to spend money, you'll be better equipped to manage your finances and make informed choices.

Let's delve deeper into each point to provide more understanding of how and when to spend money wisely.

Differentiating Between Wants and Needs

As you navigate the decision-making world, you must distinguish between wants and needs. Needs such as food, clothing, and shelter are fundamental for your well-being and survival. Wants, on the other hand, are desires that enhance your life but aren't essential. Prioritizing needs over wants will help you allocate your money more effectively and avoid overspending on non-essential items.

To practice this skill, take a moment to assess your current lifestyle and spending habits. Ask yourself, "Do I need this item to stay healthy and safe?" or "Is this purchase going to bring long-term value to my life?" By taking a thoughtful approach to your spending, you'll develop a conscious consumer mindset, making it easier to avoid impulsive purchases.

Setting a Budget

Budgeting is the foundation of financial responsibility. Creating and sticking to a budget will help you understand where your money is going and lets you plan for future expenses.

In order to do this, start by listing all your sources of income, such as weekly allowances, money from chores, or monetary gifts from relatives. Then, track your regular expenses, including school supplies, extracurricular activities, and any contributions to savings.

A budget empowers you to make calculated decisions about allocating your money. It also helps you to save for specific goals, like buying a new bicycle or contributing to a charity you support.

As you grow older, your financial responsibilities will increase, so learning budgeting early on will set you up for success in managing more complex financial situations later in life.

Saving for Goals

Setting savings goals and working toward them is an excellent practice for cultivating patience and discipline. Having a clear objective for your savings helps you stay motivated and on track with your financial goals. Whether it's a toy you've had your eye on, a contribution to a charity, or building an emergency fund, each goal contributes to your financial growth and stability.

To create a savings plan, divide your money into different categories: short-term (for smaller, more immediate goals), medium-term (for larger purchases in the near future), and long-term (for significant purposes that may take months or years to achieve).

This organized approach to saving enables you to track your progress and celebrate each milestone reached.

Prioritizing Value and Quality

When considering a purchase, especially for clothes or gadgets, it's crucial to prioritize value and quality over price. While something may seem like a great deal initially, cheaper items might wear out quickly or not function as well as higher-quality alternatives.

Making informed decisions based on value and durability ensures that your purchases serve you well over an extended period.

One way to determine value and quality is by comparing product reviews and brands. Seek out products with positive feedback from other consumers and a reputation for reliability. Moreover, opt for items with clear return or warranty policies, showing that the manufacturer stands behind their product's quality.

Researching Before Purchasing

Doing research before making a purchase is a skill that can save you both money and disappointment.

You can easily find online information and reviews about almost any product or service. Before buying a new game, a book, or even a gift for someone else, take the time to read reviews and learn about the item's features and benefits.

Additionally, consider seeking advice from family members, friends, or teachers. Their personal experiences can provide valuable insights and help you make well-informed decisions. Remember, knowledge is power, and being well-informed about your purchases empowers you to be a smart spender.

Delaying Impulse Purchases

Resisting impulse purchases is a challenging yet essential aspect of smart spending. Advertisements and persuasive marketing techniques can make products seem irresistible, but learning to pause and reflect before buying can prevent buyer's remorse.

When you strongly feel the urge to buy something on a whim, employ the "30-day rule."

The "30-day rule" involves waiting for 30 days before making the purchase. During this time, assess whether the item is necessary or if the initial excitement has faded. By the end of the waiting period, you may find that you no longer desire the item as much, allowing you to make a more rational decision about spending your money on it.

Recognizing Value in Experiences

While material possessions can bring temporary happiness, experiences often provide lasting memories and personal growth. Recognizing the value of experiences over things can lead to more fulfilling and meaningful spending decisions.

Instead of solely focusing on acquiring possessions, consider allocating a portion of your budget to experiences, such as attending concerts, going on nature hikes, or trying out new activities.

Experiences enrich your life and offer opportunities for learning and self-discovery. They allow you to build connections with others and create cherished memories that stay with you long after the moment has passed. Moreover, shared experiences with friends and family can strengthen bonds and provide a sense of belonging.

By using the skills mentioned in this chapter, you'll become a confident and responsible decision-maker when spending money.

Understanding the difference between your wants and needs, budgeting, setting goals for saving, prioritizing quality, researching before purchasing, delaying impulse buys, and valuing experiences will lead you toward financial independence and a fulfilling life.

With these skills, you can make the most of your resources and achieve your economic aspirations in the future. Embrace these skills, and remember that learning to manage your money wisely is a lifelong journey of growth and empowerment.

Why did the scale become a great decision-maker?
Because it was always able to weigh the "pros" and "cons"!

Chapter 14

Social Decisions

Have you ever given a lot of thought about how your decisions affect yourself and those around you? This is where social decisions come into play.

Social decisions are choices that impact our relationships with others.

They require us to consider the feelings and needs of other people. Learning to make good social decisions is an important skill that can help us build strong friendships, resolve conflicts, and create a positive and inclusive community.

One key aspect of social decision-making is empathy. Empathy means being able to put yourself in someone else's shoes to understand how they might feel.

It's important to consider how our choices might affect others emotionally when making social decisions. For example, if you have a sad friend, choosing to spend time with them and offer support shows empathy and can make a big difference in their day.

Another important aspect of social decision-making is considering the needs of the group. When working in a team or participating in group activities, making decisions that benefit everyone involved is crucial. This means listening to different perspectives, compromising, and finding solutions for everyone.

For example, suppose your class is planning a field trip. In that case, it's important to consider everyone's preferences and find an enjoyable destination for the whole group.

Social decisions also involve understanding and respecting different cultures, backgrounds, and beliefs. We live in a diverse world, and making inclusive decisions can help create a harmonious and accepting society.

This means being open-minded, treating others with kindness and respect, and celebrating our differences.

Remember, making social decisions may not always be easy, and sometimes we might make mistakes. However, by learning from our experiences and reflecting on the consequences of our choices, we can grow and become better decision-makers.

Social decisions are choices that impact our relationships with others and require empathy, consideration of the group's needs, and respect for diversity.

Developing our social decision-making skills can create a positive and inclusive community where everyone feels valued and heard.

So, let's remember to think not just about ourselves but also about how our decisions can make a difference in the lives of others.

Deciding Who to Be Friends With

Friends are a valuable part of our lives. They are the people we choose to spend time with, share our secrets, and have fun with. But have you ever wondered how to choose the right friends?

Making smart choices about who to be friends with is an essential skill that can bring you happiness and support throughout your life.

When deciding who to be friends with, it's important to consider the qualities you value in a friend. Do you want someone who is kind, trustworthy, and respectful? Or someone who shares your interests and makes you feel good about yourself.

Take time to write down the qualities you think are important in a friend. This will help you identify the people you want to be friends with.

Remember, having different friends for different activities or interests is okay. You might have friends at school, in your neighborhood, or from extracurricular activities like sports or music. Each friendship can bring something unique to your life, so don't be afraid to explore different kinds of friendships.

But how do you actually make friends?

One way is by being friendly and approachable. Smile and say hello to new people. Start conversations and show genuine interest in getting to know them. Remember to be yourself and let your true personality shine through.

When you are authentic, you attract friends who appreciate you for who you are.

Sometimes, you may encounter people who don't treat you well or make you uncomfortable. It's important to trust your instincts in these situations. If someone consistently hurts your feelings, disrespects you, or pressures you into doing things you don't want to do, it may be time to reconsider the friendship. It's okay to distance yourself from people who don't bring positivity into your life.

Lastly, being a good friend is as important as choosing good friends. Treat others with kindness, respect, and honesty. Be there for your friends when they need support, and listen to their feelings. Remember that friendship is a two-way street, and giving as much as you receive is important.

Choosing friends is a vital decision-making skill to help you build solid and meaningful relationships. By considering the qualities you value in a friend, being approachable, and trusting your instincts, you can surround yourself with friends who bring joy and positivity into your life.

Remember, friendships should be based on respect, kindness, and shared interests, and being a good friend is just as important as choosing good friends.

Handling Conflicts With Peers

Conflicts with our friends and peers are a common part of life. It's normal to have disagreements and differences of opinion, but knowing how to handle these conflicts respectfully and positively is important. In this section, you will learn some valuable skills to help resolve conflicts with your peers effectively.

Listen and Understand

Listening to the other person's perspective is crucial when a conflict arises. Try to understand their point of view and why they may feel the way they do. This will help you find common ground and work towards a solution you can agree on. When you listen to understand what is being said, instead of listening simply to respond, you open the door to empathy and a more meaningful conversation.

Communicate Calmly

Instead of losing your temper or shouting, express your thoughts and feelings calmly.

Use "I" statements to explain how their actions or words made you feel. For example, say, "I felt hurt when you didn't include me in the game," instead of blaming and saying, "You're so mean for leaving me out!"

Find a Compromise

Conflict resolution often requires finding a middle ground. Look for solutions that can satisfy both parties.

For instance, if you and your friend can't agree on which game to play, suggest taking turns or finding a new game you can both enjoy.

Apologize and Forgive

Sometimes, we can make mistakes or hurt other people unintentionally. This can happen when we fail to consider everything fully.

If you realize you're in the wrong, apologize sincerely.

Likewise, if your friend apologizes to you, be open to forgiving them. Remember, forgiveness allows for healing and rebuilding friendships.

Seek Help if Needed

If you find it challenging to resolve a conflict alone, don't hesitate to seek help from a trusted adult. They can offer guidance and support to find a resolution that benefits everyone involved.

Learning how to handle conflicts with your peers is an important life skill. You can positively resolve conflicts by using active listening, effective communication, compromise, and forgiveness. Conflicts are opportunities for growth and understanding, and handling them with maturity will help you build stronger and healthier relationships with your friends.

***

"You are free to make choices,
but you are not free from the consequences of those choices."
- Anonymous

Chapter 15

Problem-Solving and Decision-Making

Are you ready to become a problem-solving superstar?

Problem-solving is a skill we use every day, whether we are trying to decide what game to play, how to finish a project, or even how to handle a disagreement with a friend.

By learning problem-solving skills, you can become better equipped to tackle challenges and make smart choices.

So, what exactly is problem-solving? Well, it's like being a detective. When a problem arises, you become a detective who gathers clues, investigates different options, and finds the best solution. It's a fun and creative process that helps you think critically and make informed decisions.

To become a problem-solving star, you must follow a few basic steps.

First, identify the problem. Is it a math puzzle you can't solve, a conflict with a sibling, or a challenge at school? Once you know the problem, it's time to gather information. Talk to others, do research, or brainstorm ideas. The more information you have, the better!

Next, it's time to come up with possible solutions. This is where your creativity shines! Be bold and think outside the box and consider different perspectives. Write down all the potential solutions and evaluate each one. What are the pros and cons? Which option seems the most promising?

After evaluating the solutions, it's time to make a decision. Choose the solution that best fits the problem and aligns with your values. Remember, your decision should be based on what you think is right, not what others expect of you.

Finally, put your decision into action! Take steps to solve the problem, and be bold and adjust your approach if needed. Problem-solving is not always a one-time thing; sometimes, it requires patience and perseverance.

This chapter will explore various problem-solving techniques that will sharpen your decision-making skills.

Get ready to become a problem-solving champion and make smart problem-solving choices that will shape your future!

Understanding the Connection Between Problems and Decisions

In life, we often face different problems that need our attention. Whatever the situation, it's important to understand that every problem connects to making decisions.

Let's start by understanding what a problem is. A problem is something that needs to be solved or a situation that needs to be improved. Problems can come in many shapes and sizes, often requiring us to decide to find the best solution.

Making decisions, on the other hand, is the process of choosing one option over another. It involves thinking about the possible outcomes and considering the consequences before making a choice. Decisions can be tough, but they help solve problems and guide us toward the best possible outcome.

The connection between problems and decisions is like a puzzle. When we face a problem, we need to gather information, think about different options, and evaluate the advantages and disadvantages of each choice. This process helps us make informed decisions that can lead to solving the problem.

For example, imagine you need help figuring out what to do during your free time. You could watch TV, play video games, or read a book. To make the best decision, consider each option's consequences. Watching TV might be entertaining, but it may not be as beneficial for your mind as reading a book. By exploring the advantages and disadvantages of each choice, you can make a decision that will help solve your problem of finding something to do.

Understanding the connection between problems and decisions is an important skill to develop. It helps us become better problem-solvers and allows us to make choices that will lead to positive outcomes. By practicing decision-making skills, we can become more confident in facing and solving problems.

So, the next time you encounter a problem, take a moment to think about the different options and their consequences. By making informed decisions, you'll be well on your way to becoming a smart problem solver.

Developing Problem-Solving Skills

This section will explore how to approach and solve problems effectively, as this is an essential skill that helps us make smart choices and overcome challenges in our daily lives.

So, what exactly is problem-solving? Well, it's a process of finding solutions to difficulties or obstacles. Whether it is a math problem, a conflict with a friend, or a tricky situation at school, problem-solving skills can help us confidently navigate these challenges.

The first step in problem-solving is understanding the problem. Take a moment to define what the problem is clearly. Sometimes, problems can be overwhelming, but breaking them down into smaller parts makes them more manageable. Remember, every problem has a solution!

Next, it's time to brainstorm possible solutions. Think creatively and come up with as many ideas as possible. Don't worry about whether they are good or bad at this stage; just let your imagination run wild! After generating several options, evaluate each one by examining the pros and cons of each proposed solution, and determine which one is most likely to solve the problem effectively.

Once you have chosen a solution, it's time to take action! Implement your chosen solution and see how it works. If it doesn't solve the problem completely, don't be discouraged. Problem-solving is an iterative process, meaning you might need to go back to the drawing board and try another solution.

Remember, every attempt brings you closer to finding the right solution.

Lastly, reflect on your problem-solving process. What did you learn from this experience? Did your solution work? If not, what could you do differently next time? Learning from your mistakes and celebrating successes will help you become a better problem solver.

Remember, developing problem-solving skills takes practice. The more you engage in problem-solving, the better you will become at it. So, embrace challenges, think creatively, and never give up! With these skills, you can conquer any problem that comes your way.

In the next section, we will delve deeper into the concept of decision-making and explore how it ties into problem-solving. So, stay tuned and get ready to become a confident decision-maker!

Using the Decision-Making Process for Solving Problems

Have you ever faced a difficult problem without knowing how to solve it? Well, worry no more! This section will explore the decision-making process and how it can help you solve problems effectively. So, get ready to become a problem-solving star!

As you have already learned, decision-making is a step-by-step approach that helps us make smart choices. It consists of five simple steps: identifying the problem, gathering information, exploring options, deciding, and taking action.

The first step is identifying the problem. This means understanding the problem and why it must be solved. For example, you're having trouble with a math problem. The problem is that you need to learn how to solve it and figure out how to understand it better.

The second step is gathering information. This means finding out everything you can about the problem. In our math problem example, ask your teacher for extra help, search online for tutorials, or talk to a friend who is good at math.

Next, it's time to explore options. This means coming up with different ways to solve the problem. For our math problem, try using a different strategy, asking a classmate for help, or even visualization techniques to solve the problem.

Once you have a few options, it's time to decide. This means choosing the best option based on the information you gathered. You might try a combination of strategies or ask your teacher for more guidance.

Lastly, you need to take action. This means putting your decision into practice and seeing if it solves the problem. In our math problem example, you would apply the chosen strategy and see if it helps you progress in your mathematical studies.

Remember, decision-making is a valuable tool that can be used in many areas of your life, not just problem-solving. You can become a more confident and effective decision-maker by following these steps.

So, the next time you encounter a problem, don't panic! Just use the decision-making process to guide you toward finding a solution. You'll become a star at making smart choices and solving problems easily with practice!

Examples of Problem-Solving Using Decision-Making Skills

We often encounter problems that require us to make decisions. Sometimes these problems can seem tricky or overwhelming, but we can tackle them head-on with the right decision-making skills and find the best solutions. Let's explore a few examples of problem-solving using decision-making.

Imagine you and your friends plan a picnic, but the weather forecast predicts rain. You all have different ideas about what to do. One friend suggests going to an indoor play center, another suggests rescheduling the picnic for another day, and you think of having a movie night at someone's house.

As previously discussed, in order to make the best decision, you could use a decision-making tool called "pros and cons." This involves listing the advantages and disadvantages of each option. Doing this lets you think about each suggestion's benefits and drawbacks and ultimately decide on the best alternative.

Another example could be if you are saving up your allowance to buy a new toy. You have two options: buy the toy now or save the money for a few more weeks to get a bigger and better toy. To make this decision, you can use a decision-making tool called "weighted criteria."

First, you identify the factors that are important to you, such as the toy's size, price, and features. Then, you assign a weight to each factor to reflect its importance. By comparing the options based on these criteria, you will be able to make an informed decision that aligns with your preferences and goals.

Lastly, let's consider a scenario where you are trying to decide which extracurricular activity to participate in. You have many options, such as joining a sports team, learning a musical instrument, or taking art classes. To make this decision, you can use a decision-making tool called "decision matrix."

This involves creating a table with different activities listed as rows and criteria (like time commitment, interest, and cost) as columns. You can compare the options by rating each activity based on how well it meets each criterion and decide which suits your interests and circumstances.

Remember, decision-making is an essential skill that we all need to develop. By using decision-making tools like "pros and cons," "weighted criteria," and "decision matrix," we can solve problems effectively and make informed choices. So the next time you face a problem, consider the options and use these tools to guide your decision-making.

***

Why did the cookie go to school to learn about choices?
Because it wanted to be a smart cookie when making decisions!

Chapter 16

Become a Decision-Maker Superhero

Before exploring ways to become a decision-maker superhero, let's recap what you have learned about developing essential decision-making skills!

First, we discussed the importance of identifying the problem or decision we must make. Remember, it's crucial to understand what the issue is before trying to find a solution. We learned that recognizing the problem is the first step toward making a smart choice.

Next, we explored the concept of brainstorming. Brainstorming is a fun and creative way to come up with possible solutions to our problems. We discovered there are no wrong answers during this process, and we should encourage ourselves and others to think outside the box.

After brainstorming, we discussed the significance of evaluating our options. We learned how to weigh the different pros and cons of each option. By doing this, we can make more informed decisions that align with our values and goals.

Then, we delved into the importance of seeking advice from others. We discovered that asking for help and listening to different perspectives is okay. Getting input from friends, family, or teachers can provide valuable insights and help us see things differently.

Lastly, we explored the concept of making a decision and taking action. We learned that it's time to choose after evaluating our options and considering advice. We learned that it's essential to trust ourselves and have confidence in our decision-making abilities.

Remember, decision-making is a skill that takes practice. As you face more decisions in life, you will become better at making smart choices. It's okay to make mistakes along the way, as they are opportunities for learning and growth.

In this exciting adventure, you will learn how your decisions are like the actions of superheroes, capable of making a significant impact on your life and the lives of others. Just like superheroes save the day, your choices can create ripples of change, shaping your future and leaving a mark on the world around you.

Imagine yourself as a mighty superhero with the power to make choices that can bring about positive transformations. Every decision you make is like wielding a magical superpower, and with great power comes great responsibility. So, put on your hero cape and explore how you can become a decision-maker superhero!

The Power of Your Choices

As a young superhero, you can uniquely shape your destiny through your decisions. Each choice you make has a consequence, whether big or small. Just like superheroes consider the impact of their actions on the world, you must reflect on the implications of your choices. Will your decision bring joy or sadness, help or hurt, build or break? By embracing the power of your choices, you become a force for positive change.

Unleash Your Super Values

Superheroes have a strong moral compass, guiding them to uphold justice and do what's right. Similarly, you have your own super values - honesty, kindness, respect, and more. Embrace these values as your guiding stars, leading you to make decisions that align with your superhero identity. Whenever faced with a tough choice, consult your super values to find the path to make you a true hero.

The Quest for Integrity

Every superhero faces challenges that test their integrity, and so will you. As you journey through life, you'll encounter situations where you must choose between what's easy and right. It's during these moments that your integrity will shine. Remember, being a superhero means making choices that align with your values, even when it's complicated.

The Ripple Effect

Just like superheroes' actions have a ripple effect on the world, your choices can impact the lives of others in surprising ways. A simple act of kindness can inspire others to spread joy, while a negative choice can bring sadness. By understanding the ripple effect of your decisions, you'll recognize the immense power you hold to create a chain reaction of goodness.

The Hero's Journey

Every superhero embarks on a heroic journey, facing trials and tribulations. Similarly, your decision-making journey is a hero's quest filled with challenges and lessons.

Embrace the journey with courage and a growth mindset. Learn from your successes and mistakes, for they will mold you into a confident and wiser decision-maker.

Embracing Imperfection

Superheroes are not without flaws, and neither are you. It's essential to acknowledge that making perfect decisions all the time is impossible.

Like superheroes, you may stumble, but you will rise again, learn from your experiences, and become even more resilient.

The Heroic Impact

Every day is an opportunity to be a hero.

Small acts of kindness, helping others, and standing up for what's right are all heroic actions. As a decision-making hero, you can spread positivity and make the world a better place with each choice you make.

Remember that your choices hold the potential to make a lasting impact on your life and the lives of others. With your super values as your guiding light, you have the power to be a real-life hero in the decisions you make.

The world awaits your heroic choices, so unleash the superhero within and make each decision a force for good!

Empowering You to Make Smart Choices

Decision-making is an essential skill you must develop from an early age. Let's explore more exciting ways to supercharge your decision-making skills and boost your confidence in making smart choices.

Building this superpower will help you feel more capable and ready to take on any challenge that comes your way. Let's look into some helpful techniques to become even better decision-makers!

So, how can you become a champion decision-maker? It's easier than you might think!

Below are some practical tips to help you develop and nurture your decision-making skills.

Superhero Consequences

Think of your decisions like a superhero's actions! Just like superheroes save the day, your choices can greatly impact yourself and others. So, when you make decisions, imagine how they can create positive changes and make the world a better place!

Time Travel Scenarios

Hop into a time machine and travel to the future! Imagine the outcomes of different choices you could make. Will it lead to exciting adventures or unexpected challenges? By imagining the future, you can pick the best path that aligns with your dreams and goals.

Embrace Your Inner Captain Courage

Captain Courage is a brave character who trusts their instincts! Tap into your Captain Courage and listen to your inner voice. Your gut feeling can be a reliable guide in making choices with confidence so the sooner you get to know and understand it, the sooner you will have a trustworthy resource always on your side.

Awesome Decision Diary

Keep an awesome decision diary where you write down your choices, the reasons behind them, and how you felt after. Here you can include information about how the decision turned out and any thoughts you may have to track your progress, learn from your experiences, and gain valuable insights into your decision-making patterns.

By maintaining this diary, you create a powerful tool for self-reflection and growth. It serves as a guide to navigate through challenges by identifying potential pitfalls and areas for improvement and allows you to celebrate your successes, understand what led to positive outcomes, and replicate those strategies in the future.

Seek Guidance from Wise Wizards

Find wise wizards - parents, teachers, or older siblings. These magical mentors have a lot of wisdom to share! Talking to them can provide valuable insights and guidance when unsure about a decision.

Risks and Rewards Adventure

Every decision involves risks and rewards, just like an exciting adventure! Learn to balance both by thinking about what you might gain and what you need to be careful about. By understanding risks, you'll be a master decision-maker!

Superheros Learning From Mistakes

Even superheroes make mistakes, but they learn and grow from them! When you make a decision that doesn't turn out as planned, see it as a chance to learn and do better next time. It's all part of your superhero journey!

Galaxy of Diverse Perspectives

Imagine a galaxy of diverse perspectives - each star representing a different idea. Explore these ideas and listen to others' thoughts. Embracing different viewpoints will help you make well-rounded decisions.

Quest for Goals

Set your goals like a quest!

As you make decisions, think about how they can lead you closer to achieving your goals and dreams. With each choice, you're one step closer to becoming the hero of your story!

Building confidence in your choices will make you unstoppable as you tackle any challenge with bravery and intelligence.

Use these amazing techniques to unlock your decision-making superpower! Remember, you have the power within you to be a fearless decision-maker and create a future filled with greatness!

By developing your decision-making skills, you'll become more self-reliant, confident, and ready to face any challenge that comes your way. Remember, every decision you make is an opportunity for growth.

One of the key factors in receiving ongoing support and guidance for decision-making is having a strong support system. This includes your parents, teachers, and friends who can offer advice and help you evaluate the pros and cons of different choices.

Never hesitate to reach out to them whenever you need assistance or have questions about a decision you need to make.

In addition, it is so important to develop good communication skills.

Expressing your thoughts, concerns, and fears openly and honestly with trusted adults can help you gain valuable insights and perspectives. Remember, seeking guidance is not a sign of weakness; it shows strength and maturity.

Remember, the journey of decision-making is exciting and filled with endless opportunities.

By seeking ongoing support and guidance, practicing, reflecting, and maintaining a growth mindset, you will develop strong decision-making skills that will serve you well throughout your life.

So, let's soar to new heights and embrace the magic of becoming a true decision-making superhero!

*"Believe in yourself and your decisions.
Your heart knows what's best for you."*
- Anonymous

Chapter 17

A Test of Friendship and Ethical Choices

In the charming town of Brookville, best friends Sarah and Thomas were admired for their kindness and honesty. One day, Thomas accidentally damaged a valuable item belonging to another student, Lucy. Troubled by his mistake, Thomas confided in Sarah, seeking advice. Sarah knew they couldn't ignore what happened and encouraged Thomas to take responsibility for his actions.

Sarah understood Thomas's fear of the consequences and struggled with her conscience. She wanted to support her friend but also believed in doing what was right. As the days passed,

Sarah saw how the incident affected Lucy and couldn't bear to ignore it.

One evening, by the riverbank, Sarah talked to Thomas about her feelings, explaining that true friendship means supporting each other in making the right choices, even when difficult. With Sarah's support, they decided to confess to their teacher and face the consequences together.

Their teacher appreciated their honesty and helped them make amends to Lucy. Surprisingly, Lucy showed understanding and compassion, admiring their courage to do what was right.

Sarah and Thomas's decision to prioritize honesty was a powerful example of the importance of doing the right thing, even in difficult situations. Their genuine friendship and willingness to face the consequences together inspired their peers to value integrity and trust in their relationships. Their experience taught them that true friendship can withstand challenges when built on a foundation of honesty and respect.

Ethics is a big word, but it's all about understanding right and wrong and making good choices. Just like superheroes have a code of ethics to help them make the right decisions, you can also have your own code of ethics to guide your everyday lives.

At its core, ethics is about doing the right thing, even when no one is watching. It's about being honest and fair and treating others with respect and kindness. When we make ethical choices, we are the best versions of ourselves.

Sometimes, it can be hard to know the right thing to do. That's why it's important to consider our actions' consequences. Before making a decision, we should ask ourselves, "How will my choice affect others?" By considering the impact on others, we can decide on choices that will lead to positive outcomes for everyone involved.

Another essential aspect of ethics is empathy, which means putting ourselves in someone else's shoes. When we understand how others might feel, making considerate and compassionate choices becomes easier. For example, if we see someone being bullied, we can choose to stand up for them because we know how it would feel to be treated unkindly.

Ethics also teaches us to take responsibility for our actions. When we make a mistake, it's important to own up to it and try to make things right. This shows integrity, which means doing the right thing even when it's complicated.

Considering the above short story, it's time to explore making ethical choices.

***

Why did the pencil always make good decisions?
Because it had a sharp mind!

Chapter 18

Making Ethical Choices

When it comes to decision-making, it is crucial to think about what is best for ourselves and what is fair and right. This is called making ethical choices.

Ethical choices are decisions that align with our values and morals, and they help us become responsible and compassionate individuals. This chapter will explore how to make ethical choices and why they are important.

Firstly, let's understand what ethics are.

Ethics guide our behavior and help us determine right from wrong. Our families, communities, and personal beliefs shape these principles. Making ethical choices means considering how our actions affect others and choosing the fair, just, and respectful option.

A critical aspect of making ethical choices is empathy. Empathy means understanding how others feel.

When we empathize, we can put ourselves in someone else's shoes and consider how our decisions might impact them. For example, if we find a lost wallet, an ethical choice would be to return it to its owner because we would want someone to do the same for us if we were in that situation.

Another important concept to consider is honesty. Being honest means telling the truth and being trustworthy. Making ethical choices often involves being honest with ourselves and others, even when difficult. For instance, if we break something, a moral choice is to admit our mistake and take responsibility for it.

Making ethical choices also requires us to consider our actions' consequences.

What might happen if we choose one option over another? Will it harm someone or benefit them? By considering the potential outcomes, we can make decisions that prioritize the well-being of others.

It is essential to remember that making ethical choices is a lifelong journey. Our values and understanding of right and wrong may change as we grow.

What is important is that we always strive to make fair, just, and respectful choices for others.

What Exactly Are Ethics?

Ethics guide us to make good decisions and do the right thing. They help us understand what is fair, just, and morally correct.

Imagine ethics as a compass that points us in the right direction when faced with difficult choices.

When discussing ethics, we discuss how we should behave and treat others. It's like having a rulebook for being a good person. Having a solid ethical foundation helps us make thoughtful decisions and consider our choices' impact on ourselves and those around us.

Let's explore some important ethical values that can guide our decision-making process:

Honesty

Being honest means telling the truth and not deceiving others. It is essential to be truthful, even if it means admitting mistakes.

Respect

Respecting others means treating everyone with kindness, empathy, and fairness. We should value diversity and treat others the way we want to be treated.

Responsibility

Being responsible means taking ownership of our actions and their consequences. We should consider how our decisions affect others and take responsibility for our choices.

Integrity

Having integrity means standing up for what is right, even when difficult. It means being true to our values and not compromising our beliefs.

Compassion

Compassion involves showing empathy and care toward others. It means being understanding and supportive, especially when someone is going through a tough time.

Fairness

Fairness means treating everyone equally and without bias. It involves giving everyone a fair chance and not favoring one person over another.

Understanding and practicing these ethical values helps us become responsible decision-makers. Remember, as children, you have the power to make a difference in the world. You can create a kinder and more considerate society by embracing ethics and making smart choices. Considering these principles, we can make choices that benefit us and contribute positively to our families, friends, and communities.

You've probably heard the saying, "Treat others how you would like to be treated," so remember this when considering any options that could affect somebody else.

So, let's strive to make ethical decisions every day and be the change we want to see in the world!

Considering the Impact of Decisions on Others

When making decisions, it's always important to consider how our choices can affect others. This is called considering the impact of decisions on others. Making decisions considering the well-being and feelings of those around us is essential to help us navigate life successfully.

Imagine you and your friends are playing a game, and one suggests a rule you don't like. You have a decision to make. If you say no without considering how it might make your friend feel, it could hurt their feelings and ruin the fun for everyone. Instead think about their perspective and find a compromise that makes everyone happy. In that case, it can strengthen your friendship and make the game more enjoyable.

Considering the impact of decisions on others means putting yourself in someone else's shoes. It's about empathy and understanding. When we take the time to think about how our choices can affect others, we become more aware of the consequences of our actions.

For example, you have a younger sibling who looks up to you. You have the power to influence them with your decisions. They might follow your lead and make similar choices if you make good choices. But if you make poor choices, they might think it's okay to do the same.

By considering the impact on your sibling, you can strive to be a positive role model and make decisions that will inspire them to do the right thing.

Considering the impact of decisions on others also helps us build stronger relationships. When we take the time to understand how our choices can affect our friends, family, and even strangers, we show them that we care.

This builds trust and respect, making our relationships stronger and more meaningful.

Remember, every decision we make has the power to affect others. By considering the impact of our choices on others, we become more compassionate, thoughtful, and responsible individuals. So, next time you need to make a decision, consider how it might affect those around you.

Your consideration and empathy will make a world of difference in the lives of others and your own life.

Evaluating the Ethical Implications of Choices

When making decisions, it's important to consider what is best for us and what is right. This is where ethics comes into play. This section will explore the ethical implications of our choices and how to make decisions that align with our values.

Sometimes, we face choices that may seem easy initially, but when we dig deeper, we realize they have ethical implications.

For example, imagine finding a wallet on the ground. You have two options: keep the money or try to find the owner. While keeping the money may seem tempting, it is not an ethical choice. Taking the time to find the owner and returning the wallet is the right thing to do.

To evaluate the ethical implications of our choices, you need to ask yourself some important questions.

Firstly, is it fair? Will your decision treat others with respect and equality? Secondly, is it honest? Does your choice involve telling the truth or being transparent? Next, you should consider if it is respectful. Will your decision show kindness and consideration toward others?

Lastly, it would be best if you thought about the consequences. Will your choice positively or negatively impact you and those around you?

Let's take another example. Imagine you and your friends are playing a game, and one of them is cheating. You have a choice to make. If you ignore the cheating, you are not being fair to others who are playing honestly. So do you speak up and confront your friend about their cheating?

In that case, you make an ethical choice by standing up for fairness and honesty.

By evaluating the ethical implications of your choices, you become more responsible decision-makers, where you can develop a strong moral compass and build character. This helps you make choices that align with your values and treat others fairly and respectfully.

Making ethical choices may not always be easy, but it is always worth it.

It shows that you are a trustworthy, respectful, and considerate individual. So, let's always strive to make choices that benefit us and make the world a better place for everyone.

"Every choice you make, big or small, shapes the person you become. Choose wisely!"
- Anonymous

Chapter 19

Independent Decision-Making

You are at a crucial stage of your development, beginning to make more independent choices. Having the right tools and resources to help you navigate this exciting and sometimes challenging phase of your life is essential. This is the same as having the right equipment for school, sports, or any other worthwhile activity you want to do well.

The more you understand, the more experience you gain, the better you will become.

Understanding the Power of Choice

Every choice we make has consequences, whether big or small. Being empowered to make smart choices begins with understanding the power you hold. As a young person, you can shape your future and create positive outcomes by making wise decisions. This section will explore how even seemingly insignificant choices can significantly impact your life.

In the exciting journey of growing up, you face numerous daily choices and decisions. From what to wear to school to picking activities and even making choices about friends, decision-making is an essential skill you must develop from an early age. Learning to make smart choices helps you become more independent, builds your confidence, and sets you on the path to success.

So, how can you become a champion decision-maker? It's easier than you might think! Below are some practical tips to help you develop and nurture your decision-making skills.

Gather Information

As you know, before making any decision, you must take the time to gather all the relevant information. For instance, if you decide what activity to join after school, research and learn about the options available. Ask your friends, teachers, and parents for their opinions and experiences. As you know, the more information you have, the better equipped you'll be to make an informed choice.

As you grow older, the complexity of the decisions you face will likely increase. Research becomes even more critical when choosing a school, a career path, or even deciding where to live. Utilize the internet, visit campuses, talk to professionals in your fields of interest, and consider your long-term goals.

Comprehensive research ensures you make choices that align with your values and aspirations.

Weigh the Pros and Cons

Once you have collected the necessary information, write down the pros and cons of each option. Think about the advantages and disadvantages of each choice and how they align with your personal values and goals. This exercise will help you see the bigger picture and make a more balanced decision.

As you face more complex decisions, learning to weigh the pros and cons becomes an essential analytical skill. Creating a decision matrix can be helpful, where you assign weights to different factors based on their importance and evaluate each option accordingly. This structured approach assists you in making more well-rounded choices.

Trust Your Instincts

Sometimes, despite careful analysis, you may still feel uncertain about a decision. In such cases, trust your instincts. Your gut feeling often reflects your inner wisdom and can guide you toward making the right choice.

As you gain more life experiences, your instincts become sharper, and you'll learn to trust your intuition in challenging situations. Intuition can offer valuable insights when the logical aspects of decision-making aren't enough. However, remember to balance intuition with rational thinking for the best possible outcomes.

Take Responsibility

Remember, decision-making is a learning process. It's okay to make mistakes. When you do, take responsibility for them, learn from them, and move forward.

Through all these experiences, you'll grow and become a better decision-maker.

As you face more significant decisions in adulthood, acknowledging and learning from mistakes becomes even more crucial. Owning up to your good and bad decisions shows maturity and resilience. It allows you to adapt and refine your decision-making approach, leading to more successful outcomes in the future.

Seek Guidance

Don't be afraid to seek guidance from trusted adults. Parents, teachers, or mentors can provide valuable insights and help you navigate complex decisions. Their guidance can help you consider different perspectives and make more informed choices.

As you grow older, seeking advice from mentors or professionals in your desired fields can be instrumental in making career-related decisions. Engaging in informational interviews and networking can provide valuable guidance, introduce you to new opportunities, and offer mentorship supporting your long-term goals.

Embrace Lifelong Learning

In your journey of learning about decision-making skills, it is essential to understand that making smart choices is not a one-time event.

It is a lifelong process that requires ongoing support and guidance. Just like any skill, decision-making can be honed and improved with time and practice.

Embracing a growth mindset, where you view challenges as opportunities to learn and grow, will serve you well throughout life. Be open to new experiences, continuously seek knowledge, and stay curious about the world around you.

As you encounter diverse situations, your decision-making abilities will adapt and strengthen, helping you overcome obstacles and embrace success.

By developing your decision-making skills, you'll become more self-reliant, confident, and ready to face any challenge that comes your way.

Every decision you make is an opportunity for growth. So, embrace it, trust yourself, and make smart choices that will shape your future!

These skills will help you succeed in the present and lay the foundation for a fulfilling and purposeful life ahead. Remember, the choices you make today shape the person you become tomorrow, so embrace the journey of decision-making with confidence and enthusiasm!

***

Why did the puzzle piece become a pro at making choices?
Because it knew that decisions, like puzzles, require putting the right pieces together!

Chapter 20

Impulsive Decisions

Impulsive decisions are choices made quickly and without careful consideration of the consequences. While some spontaneous actions can lead to positive outcomes, many impulsive decisions have the potential to cause harm, regret, and complications in our lives.

In this chapter, we will explore the nature of impulsive decisions, underlying triggers, and strategies to cultivate a more thoughtful decision-making process.

Impulsive decisions may offer immediate gratification, but they often lack the consideration of long-term consequences.

By understanding the triggers of impulsivity and cultivating thoughtful decision-making, you can navigate life's challenges with greater wisdom and resilience.

Embrace the power of pausing, reflecting, and assessing before acting, ensuring that your choices align with your values and lead to positive short and long-term outcomes.

Remember, with practice, patience, and self-awareness, you can harness the art of thinking before acting and make informed decisions that contribute to a more fulfilling life.

Understanding Impulsive Decisions

Impulsivity is a natural human tendency driven by emotions, external stimuli, or our desire for instant gratification.

It can manifest in various aspects of our lives, such as impulsive spending, reacting impulsively to emotions, or making snap judgments without gathering all the necessary information.

The allure of immediate satisfaction in impulsive decisions can be tempting and often comes at the expense of long-term goals, well-being, and peace of mind. The challenge for most people lies in finding a balance between embracing spontaneity and exercising prudent judgment.

Triggers of Impulsive Decisions

Recognizing the triggers that lead to impulsive decisions is the first step in managing them effectively. A trigger, in a psychological context, refers to a stimulus or event that sets off a particular thought, emotion, or behavioral response in an individual. It's important to recognize triggers and understand their impact on our mental and emotional well-being.

Some common triggers include:

Emotional Turmoil

Intense emotions like anger, frustration, or excitement can cloud our judgment, leading us to react impulsively without considering the consequences.

Social Pressure

The desire to fit in or gain peer approval may push us to make hasty choices to please others, even if they contradict our values.

Lack of Patience

Impatience to achieve results or experience immediate rewards can lead us to make rash decisions without considering long-term consequences.

External Influences

Advertisements, social media, and societal trends can influence us to make impulsive purchases or decisions based on current fads.

Stress and Fatigue

High-stress levels and fatigue can impair our ability to think rationally, increasing the likelihood of impulsive actions.

Cultivating Thoughtful Decision-Making

Pause and Reflect

Be mindful of any emotional intensity triggered by a situation, and give yourself the time and space needed to process any emotions before finalizing your decision. Acknowledge your emotions and the desire for immediate action, but give yourself time to consider the potential outcomes.

When faced with a situation that triggers an impulse, always take a moment to pause and reflect.

Assess the Consequences

Before making a decision, weigh the short-term gains against the long-term consequences. Consider how the decision may affect your goals, relationships, and well-being.

Seek Alternatives

Explore alternative courses of action that align with your values and objectives. Evaluate different options mindfully, allowing yourself to make a well-informed decision that best serves your interests and leads to more positive outcomes in the long run.

Sleep on It

Give yourself time to sleep on significant decisions, especially those made under emotional stress. Go to bed and consider your options again in the morning. A new day can often bring a fresh perspective, and rest can help organize your thoughts and provide clarity.

Establish Priorities

Know your priorities and align your decisions accordingly. When you have a clear sense of what truly matters to you, it becomes easier to resist impulsive choices that do not support your goals.

Set Limits

If impulsive spending is a challenge, set limits on discretionary expenses. Establish and stick to a budget to avoid making financial decisions in the heat of the moment.

Seek Support

Talk to trusted friends, family members, or mentors about important decisions. Sharing your thoughts can provide valuable insights and help you see things from different perspectives.

Learning From Impulsive Choices

It's essential to remember that making an occasional impulsive decision is part of being human. If you don't learn from your mistakes, you will more than likely repeat them. Instead of dwelling on regret, focus on learning from these experiences.

Reflect on Outcomes

After making an impulsive decision, take time to reflect on the results. Analyze what went well and not so well and what you could have done differently to make a more informed choice next time.

Identify Triggers

Identify the triggers that led to the impulsive decision. By recognizing these triggers, you can develop strategies to manage them effectively in the future.

Cultivate Mindfulness

Practice mindfulness to become more aware of your thoughts, emotions, and impulses. Mindfulness helps you create space between stimuli and responses, enabling you to make more deliberate choices.

Develop Resilience

Embrace setbacks as opportunities for growth. Resilience allows you to bounce back from impulsive decisions and make more thoughtful choices.

Celebrate Thoughtful Decisions

Acknowledge and celebrate instances where you resisted impulsive choices and made thoughtful decisions. Positive reinforcement strengthens your ability to choose wisely in the future.

Impulsive decisions may provide immediate satisfaction or relief, tempting us to act without considering the potential long-term consequences. The allure of instant gratification can cloud our judgment and divert our attention from the bigger picture. While these decisions may offer short-lived benefits, they often fail to consider the ripple effects they can have on our lives and those around us.

Understanding the triggers that lead to impulsivity is crucial in controlling impulsive behavior. External factors, such as peer pressure or societal influences, can sway our decisions at the moment, pulling us away from rational thinking. Emotions, too, play a significant role in impulsive actions. Strong feelings like anger, excitement, or fear can overpower our logical reasoning and lead us to make choices that we may later regret.

To counteract impulsivity, cultivating thoughtful decision-making is essential. By becoming more self-aware and mindful of our emotions and thought processes, we can develop the capacity to step back and assess the potential outcomes before acting. Taking a moment to pause and reflect enables us to consider the ramifications of our choices and the impact they may have on our lives in the long run.

One powerful tool in combating impulsive decisions is the practice of mindfulness. Mindfulness encourages us to stay present in the moment, fully aware of our thoughts and feelings without immediate judgment. By cultivating mindfulness, we create a space between stimulus and response, allowing us to deliberate on our actions before committing to them impulsively.

The art of thinking before acting lies in the power of pausing. When faced with a challenging decision, taking a brief moment to breathe and collect your thoughts can help you gain clarity and make more informed choices. Instead of giving in to the impulse for immediate gratification, you can evaluate the situation thoroughly, considering the short-term gains and potential long-term consequences.

In this pursuit of thoughtful decision-making, aligning our choices with our values and principles is crucial. When we are clear about what truly matters to us, it becomes easier to resist impulsive temptations that may contradict our beliefs or long-term goals. Keeping our values at the forefront empowers us to make decisions that reflect our authentic selves and contribute to our personal growth and well-being.

Navigating life's challenges with greater wisdom and resilience begins with recognizing that impulsive actions can be harmful and counterproductive. By embracing the power of reflection, we can make conscious choices that steer us toward positive outcomes in the immediate and distant future. Embracing the art of thinking before acting empowers us to be more proactive and intentional in our decision-making, leading to a more fulfilling and purposeful life.

Becoming a more thoughtful decision-maker requires practice, patience, and self-awareness. Stumbling is okay along the way, as learning from our mistakes is crucial to growth. With each decision, we can evolve and make more informed choices that contribute to our personal development and pave the way for a brighter and more fulfilling future.

***

> "Life is a journey, and every decision is a step forward.
> Embrace the path you choose!"
> - Anonymous

Conclusion

The previous chapters taught you the essential skills to help you make smart decisions.

In *Smart Choices: Decision-Making for Kids*, you have discovered insights on decision-making skills that will help you become smarter and more confident in making choices. Let's recap what you've learned!

Recap of Decision-Making Skills

First, we discussed the importance of identifying the problem or decision that needs to be made. Remember, it's crucial to understand what the issue is before trying to find a solution. We learned that recognizing the problem is the first step toward making a smart choice.

Next, we explored the concept of brainstorming. Brainstorming is a fun and creative way to come up with possible solutions to our problems. We discovered that there are no wrong answers during this process, and we should encourage ourselves and others to think outside the box.

After brainstorming, we explored the significance of evaluating our options. You learned how to weigh the pros and cons of each solution and consider the possible consequences they might have. By doing this, we can make more informed decisions that align with our values and goals.

Then, we delved into the importance of seeking advice from others. We discovered that asking for help and listening to different perspectives is okay. Getting input from friends, family, or teachers can provide valuable insights and help us see things from a different angle.

Lastly, we explored the concept of making a decision and taking action. We learned that once we have evaluated our options and considered advice, it's time to make a choice. We discovered that it's essential to trust ourselves and have confidence in our decision-making abilities.

Remember, decision-making is a skill that takes practice. As you face more decisions in life, you will become better at making smart choices. It's okay to make mistakes along the way, as they are opportunities for learning and growth.

Reviewing the Decision-Making Process

This section will review the exact steps in the decision-making process. We know making decisions can sometimes be tough. Understanding the steps involved in decision-making can make you more confident in your choices.

Step 1: Identify the Decision
Step 2: Gather Information
Step 3: Consider the Alternatives
Step 4: Evaluate the Consequences
Step 5: Make a Decision
Step 6: Take Action
Step 7: Review Your Decision

Step 1: Identify the Decision

Firstly, it's crucial to identify the decision you need to make. Whether it's choosing between two games to play or deciding what hobby to pursue, understanding what decision needs to be made is the first step. You learned about the importance of understanding the problem or situation you're facing and how to Identify the key elements.

Step 2: Gather Information

Depending upon the decision you need to make, you may need to gather information to make an informed decision. Talk to friends or family members, read books, or do some research online to learn more about your options. The more information you have, the better your decision will be. Remember to ask questions, research, and seek advice from trusted adults when needed.

Step 3: Consider the Alternatives

Once you have gathered enough information, it's time to consider the alternatives. Consider the options available to you and weigh their pros and cons. This will help you narrow down your choices.

Next, we emphasized the significance of considering multiple options.

Exploring different possibilities allows you to broaden your thinking and consider alternative solutions. Don't limit yourself to only one choice – be open-minded and creative! You can make a more balanced decision by weighing the advantages and disadvantages. Always consider the short-term and long-term consequences and how they align with your values and goals.

Step 4: Evaluate the Consequences

Before making a final decision, it's important to consider the potential consequences. Think about how your decision might impact yourself and those around you. Are there any potential risks or benefits? Evaluating the consequences will help you make a more thoughtful choice. We also highlighted the value of considering your feelings and intuition. Pay attention to your gut instincts, which often guide you in the right direction. However, balancing your emotions with logical reasoning is essential to ensure a well-rounded decision.

In addition, you discovered the concept of trade-offs. Sometimes, you have to give up one thing to gain another. Understanding the trade-offs helps you prioritize and make choices that align with your priorities and values.

Step 5: Make a Decision

Now that you have gone through the previous steps, it's time to decide. Always trust your instincts and go with the option that feels most right for you. Remember, there are no right or wrong decisions, just different results, which may have positive or negative outcomes.

Step 6: Take Action

Now that you've thoughtfully decided, it's time to take action and bring your decision to life. Create a clear plan, set achievable goals, and stay confident in your decisions. Embrace challenges as learning opportunities and seek support when needed. Stay committed, evaluate your progress, and celebrate every step toward your goals.

Step 7: Review Your Decision

The final step is to review your decision. Take some time to reflect on whether your decision was best for you. Did it achieve the desired outcome? If not, what could you have done differently? This step is crucial as it helps you learn from your experiences and improve your decision-making skills for the future.

Reflecting on your decisions helps you learn from your experiences and improve your decision-making skills for future choices. Learn from your mistakes and always celebrate your successes – every decision is an opportunity for growth!

Helpful Tips

This section contains a collection of helpful tips to further empower you on your decision-making journey. These tips will elevate your decision-making, helping you become more confident, thoughtful, and resilient. From seeking ongoing support, improving communication skills, overcoming challenges, and practicing self-reflection, each tip is designed to enhance your decision-making prowess. Embrace these insights, and watch as they pave the way for a brighter and more fulfilling future, empowering you to make choices that align with your goals and values.

Ongoing Support and Guidance

A strong support system is one of the key factors in benefiting from ongoing support and guidance in your decision-making. This includes your parents, teachers, and friends, who can offer advice and help you evaluate the pros and cons of different choices. Feel free to reach out to them whenever you need assistance or have questions about a decision you need to make.

Good Communication Skills

Additionally, it is vital to develop good communication skills. Being able to express your thoughts, concerns, and fears openly and honestly with trusted adults can help you gain valuable insights and perspectives. Remember, seeking guidance isn't a sign of weakness; it's a sign of strength and maturity.

Overcoming Challenges

Making decisions can sometimes be challenging, especially when faced with peer pressure or conflicting emotions. You now understand the importance of trusting your instincts and staying true to your values. Making mistakes is a natural part of the learning process, and resilience and adaptability are crucial for growth.

Self-Reflection

Reflection is a valuable tool for learning and growth. Take time to evaluate your decisions and their outcomes. What worked well? What could have been done differently? Reflecting on your choices will help you learn from experience and make better decisions in the future.

Growth Mindset

Developing a growth mindset is also crucial. Understand that even if you make a wrong decision, it does not define you. Instead, it provides an opportunity to learn and grow. Embrace mistakes as valuable lessons and use them to make smarter choices next time so that you do not repeat the same mistakes.

By cultivating a growth mindset, you'll view challenges as stepping stones towards improvement and remain open to adapting your decision-making approach to achieve greater success in the future.

Practice

Lastly, never underestimate the power of constant practice as decision-making is a skill that can be improved with practice. Start with small choices and gradually work your way up to more significant decisions. The more you practice, the more confident and proficient you will become.

Remember, the journey of decision-making is exciting and filled with endless opportunities. By seeking ongoing support and guidance, practicing, reflecting, and maintaining a growth mindset, you will develop strong decision-making skills that will serve you well throughout your life.

Reviewing your decisions will make you more aware of the process to make even smarter choices next time. So, keep exploring, learning, and growing as you navigate life's many decisions.

You can now confidently navigate life's challenges using the decision-making skills you learned in this book.

Go out there, use your newfound knowledge, and make smart choices that will shape your future for the best!

So, what will you decide to do now?

"Trust yourself.
You have the power to make amazing decisions
and create a bright future."
- Anonymous

What Are Your Decisions?

In this section, we will explore various scenarios that require decision-making. Everything you have learned in this book will help you carefully analyze each situation and make thoughtful choices. Each scenario presents unique challenges and consequences, and your decision-making skills will be crucial in navigating them effectively.

Throughout this book, you have gained valuable knowledge to guide you in making responsible decisions in these scenarios.

Trust your judgment, consider the outcomes of your choices, and act in alignment with your values and the principles you've learned. Embrace the opportunities for growth, learning, and making a positive impact through your decision-making journey.

It's important to remember that sometimes there might not be a clear-cut right or wrong answer, but there will always be a right answer for you.

Read each scenario, and decide which option best aligns with your values and principles. Trust yourself and your ability to make choices that reflect who you are and what you believe in.

Grab a pencil, and circle each option you decide upon.

THE LOST WALLET

You find a wallet on the street containing identification and a substantial amount of money.

Option 1:   Keep the money and discard the wallet.

Option 2:   Take the wallet to the nearest police station or contact the owner if possible.

THE BROKEN VASE

While visiting a friend's house, you accidentally knock over and break a valuable vase.

Option 1:   Pretend it didn't happen and leave without mentioning it.

Option 2:   Apologize immediately, take responsibility, and offer to replace or repair the vase.

THE GOSSIP

You overhear a juicy secret about your best friend.

Option 1:   Spread the gossip to others.

Option 2:   Respect your friend's privacy and keep the secret to yourself.

***

THE LOST PET

You find a lost pet wandering in your neighborhood.

Option 1:   Ignore the pet and continue with your day.

Option 2:   Take the pet in, notify local shelters, and make efforts to find its owner.

***

THE SCHOOL BULLY

You witness a classmate being bullied by another student.

Option 1:   Ignore the situation and avoid getting involved.

Option 2: Stand up for the classmate being bullied and report the incident to a teacher or adult.

THE HOMEWORK DILEMMA

Your friend asks to copy your homework.

Option 1:   Allow your friend to copy your homework.

Option 2:   Encourage your friend to complete the work on their own and offer assistance if needed.

***

THE SHOPLIFTING INCIDENT

You see someone shoplifting in a store.

Option 1:   Pretend not to notice and continue shopping.

Option 2:   Alert a store employee or security guard about the incident.

***

THE CHEATING CLASSMATE

You witness a classmate cheating on a crucial test.

Option 1:   Ignore the cheating and focus on your own work.

Option 2:   Report the cheating to the teacher or authority figure.

THE ENVIRONMENTAL CHOICE

You are given the option to use a disposable plastic cup or a reusable one.

Option 1:   Choose a disposable plastic cup for convenience.

Option 2:   Choose a reusable cup to reduce waste and environmental impact.

***

CONFLICT WITH A FRIEND

You have a disagreement with a close friend.

Option 1:   Hold a grudge and avoid speaking to your friend.

Option 2:   Communicate openly, listen to each other's perspectives, and work towards resolving the conflict.

***

DIGITAL HURT

You receive a hurtful message or comment online.

Option 1:   Respond with anger and retaliate.

Option 2:   Take a deep breath, step away from the situation, and report or ignore the hurtful comment.

THE SAVINGS GOAL

You've been saving up for a special item, but your favorite store has a sale on a different game you like.

Option 1:   Use your savings to buy the game on sale.

Option 2:   Stick to your savings goal.

***

THE TEAM PLAYER

During a team project, your personal success could overshadow the group's success.

Option 1:   Focus solely on personal success.

Option 2:   Work together to achieve the best outcome.

***

THE PERSONAL SOCIAL MEDIA POST

You're about to post something on social media without thinking about its potential impact on others.

Option 1:   Post without considering the consequences on others.

Option 2:   Reflect on the post's impact, ensuring it's respectful and doesn't harm others.

THE GROUP PROJECT CONFLICT

During a group project your team can't agree on the best approach.

Option 1: Avoid confrontation even if you disagree with the ideas.

Option 2: Express your concerns, and work together to find a compromise.

***

THE HELPING HAND

You see someone struggling to carry heavy bags.

Option 1: Walk past without offering assistance.

Option 2: Show kindness and offer to help carry the bags.

***

THE PEER PRESSURE PARTY

Your friends invite you to a party with activities that go against your values.

Option 1: Give in to peer pressure and attend the party.

Option 2: Stay true to your values and decline the invitation, suggesting an alternative.

THE ACADEMIC DISHONESTY DILEMMA

Your classmates are planning to cheat on an upcoming test.

Option 1:   Go along with the plan to cheat.

Option 2:   Encourage your classmates to study together and avoid cheating.

***

THE CYBERBULLYING WITNESS

You come across hurtful messages online directed at one of your classmates.

Option 1:   Ignore the cyberbullying and stay out of it.

Option 2:   Offer the victim support, and report the incident.

***

THE ENVIRONMENTAL CLEANUP

While walking in the park, you notice a littered area filled with trash.

Option 1:   Walk past the littered area and assume someone else will clean it up.

Option 2:   Take the initiative to pick up and dispose of the litter.

THE BROKEN PROMISE

You promised your best friend that you would go to their birthday party, but your family plans a fun outing on the same day.

Option 1: Brush off the broken promise and hope your friend won't be too upset.

Option 2: Apologize sincerely, explain the situation to your friend, and find a way to make it up to them.

***

THE SAVING CHALLENGE

You receive money as a gift and want to buy a new toy, but your parents encourage you to save it for something you really want.

Option 1: Spend the money right away on the toy you want.

Option 2: Listen to your parents and save the money.

***

THE DECISION TO SHARE

You and a friend want the same game, but only one can afford it.

Option 1: As you have the money, buy the game for yourself.

Option 2: Suggest sharing the game and taking turns playing it.

THE TREAT TEMPTATION

You're at the store and see your favorite treat, but you've already spent your allowance.

Option 1: Ask someone else to buy the treat for you.

Option 2: Remind yourself that you've already spent your money and save the treat for another time.

***

THE BIRTHDAY DILEMMA

It's your friend's birthday, and they really want the latest game.

Option 1: Buy a cheaper gift they'll like, but it isn't the game.

Option 2: Contribute money to buy the game with other friends.

***

THE MISTAKEN IDENTITY

You accidentally spill juice on the floor during a school event, and a teacher mistakenly blames your friend for the mess.

Option 1: Stay quiet and let your friend take the blame.

Option 2: Speak up and tell the teacher the truth, explaining that your friend wasn't responsible for the spill.

THE BROKEN ITEM

You borrow your friend's favorite toy and accidentally break it at home. Your friend asks you to return it.

Option 1:   Lie and say you don't know where it is, hoping they won't be upset and will forget about it.

Option 2:   Tell your friend the truth and apologize sincerely, explaining that you accidentally broke their toy and that you'll do your best to replace it.

***

DRESS CODE DILEMMA

Your school is having a special event, and there's a dress code in place.

Option 1:   Ignore the dress code and wear whatever you want, thinking it doesn't matter.

Option 2:   Respect the dress code and choose an outfit that follows the guidelines to show respect for the event and those attending.

THE HONESTY TEST

Your teacher makes a mistake while grading your test and accidentally gives you a higher score.

Option 1: Keep quiet about the error and enjoy the higher grade.

Option 2: Approach your teacher and point out the mistake, even if it means your grade might be adjusted to the correct one.

***

THE FOOTWEAR CHOICE

You're getting ready for a fun outing with your friends but can't decide between comfortable or fashionable footwear.

Option 1: Opt for stylish shoes that may not be the most comfortable for walking or playing.

Option 2: Prioritize comfort and select shoes that will allow you to enjoy the outing without any discomfort or soreness, even if they may not be as fashionable as other options.

***

Why did the pencil break up with the eraser?
Because it couldn't make up its mind - to erase or not to erase!

Glossary

accountability: taking responsibility for something

align: to match something

analysis paralysis: inability to make a decision due to overthinking or fear

aspirations: hope or ambition of achieving something

authentic: real or genuine

benefits: helpful results or effects

biases: thoughts favoring one side of an issue over another

brainstorm: discuss a problem to come up with new ideas

budget: a spending plan

buyer's remorse: regret after buying an item

compassion: recognizing the suffering of another and offering to help if possible

conflicting: a struggle between different ideas

consumer: a customer who buys or uses something

contemplation: thinking about something deeply

credibility: the quality of being trusted or believed in

diversity: variety and the differences between people

durability: when something lasts for a long time

embodiment: giving form to an abstract idea

embrace: welcome with open arms

empathy: ability to understand what other people feel

ethical: behavior that is truthful, fair and honest

evaluate: judge the quality or relevance

exemplary: excellent behavior that deserves recognition

factors: elements or facts that can influence something

fulfillment: completion of something that brings happiness and satisfaction

gratification: a source of pleasure

harmony: being peaceful together, not arguing or fighting

honing: to practice for improvement

hypothetical: possible ideas or situations rather than actual ones

instincts: a way of behaving that is not learned

integrity: being honest and doing what is right

intuition: acting a certain way without exactly knowing why

manifest: see evidence of something appearing or happening

mind map: a diagram to organize information about a topic

mindset: an attitude or belief

moral compass: knowing what is right and wrong

obstacles: something that blocks you from moving forward

options: a point of view not based on fact

outcomes: the end result

perspective: the way you see something

preferences: when you like one thing more than another

principles: a rule or belief that guides you

procrastinate: to put off doing something

profound: feeling or experiencing something in a strong way

prudent: showing careful judgment

redemption: making good on an error or mistake

remorse: deep regret for doing wrong

reputation: general belief that other people have about you

resilient: ability to withstand setbacks and bounce back

resolve: to deal with something successfully

resonating: to produce a positive feeling or response to something

scenario: a possibility of an event

self-esteem: how we value and think about ourselves

stereotypes: oversimplified beliefs about others and how they may behave

succumbing: to accept something you didn't at first

trials and tribulations: difficult situations and unpleasant experiences

turbulent: chaotic and disordered

verify: to confirm and prove the truth

www.ingramcontent.com/pod-product-compliance
Lightning Source LLC
Chambersburg PA
CBHW021107080526
44587CB00010B/422